Little Gift

34 Tasty Morsels to Make, Package, and Give to the Special People in Your Life

by wato

Translated by Julianne Neville

One Peace
Books

Contents

wato
Little Gift: 34 Tasty Morsels to Make, Package, and Give to the Special People in Your Life

Copyright © 2011 by Sanctuary Books
Translation copyright © 2013 by One Peace Books

Originally published in 2011 by Sanctuary Books, Japan, as *Little Gift: Portable Gifts of Food for the Special People in Your Life*

First edition published by One Peace Books, 2013
1 2 3 4 5 6 7 8 9 10

Translation by Julianne Neville
Photography by Ooe Hiroyuki
Styling by U-KO
Editing by Iida Kumiko (Japanese) and Erin Canning (English)

ISBN: 978-1-935548-28-7

Printed in China

Distributed by SCB Distributors
www.scbdistributors.com

For more information, contact:
One Peace Books
43-32 22nd Street, #204
Long Island City, NY 11101
www.onepeacebooks.com

Title font: Sofia

Introduction

For special days or days you want to make special...

"It's been such a long time!"
"You mean a lot to me."
"I had some leftovers I needed to use up."
"There were these delicious-looking vegetables at the market today!"
"I remember you told me you liked this."

Whether you're visiting a friend, going to a barbecue or picnic, looking to make something you can share with your coworkers, wanting to thank someone who has done you a favor, or just because, there's nothing better than the gift of homemade food. And the stronger your feelings, the more they will shine through in the flavor. Even if you are too modest to call the simple results of your cooking "gifts," the love you put into these dishes really will transform them into spectacular gifts.

In *Little Gift*, you willl not only find a wide variety of easy-to-follow, appetizing recipes, including some traditional Japanese dishes, but also "When Giving as a Gift" ideas for attractively packaging and easily transporting the gift straight to the lucky recipient. Plus, all of the recipes are easily customizable, and the "Tasty Tips" included with each recipe share additional helpful hints.

It doesn't matter if you're a novice or a seasoned cook; once you begin cooking these dishes for others and gifting them, I think you will find that you will be giving yourself an irreplaceable gift, too.

Happy cooking!

wato

Getting Started

About the Recipes

- These dishes are indeed little gifts, so the portion sizes are on the smaller side. But you can double or triple the recipes, depending on the occasion.
- For recipes that have microwave instructions, the recommended heating time is based on a 600-watt microwave. Depending on the make of your microwave, the heating time may be longer or shorter, so adjust accordingly.
- Other cooking equipment that may be useful to have on hand: bamboo steamer, chopsticks, rice cooker (you can also cook rice in a heavy-bottomed pot with a lid), rice paddle, and sushi mat.

When Cooking

- Read the recipe over at least once in its entirety before attempting to make it. You should also read the "Tasty Tips," as there is helpful information and ideas that you may want to incorporate into the recipe.
- Always organize your cooking space so that it is clear of any obstructions and lay out your ingredients and cooking equipment in advance—doing this will greatly streamline your cooking experience.
- Remember, cleanliness is next to godliness! Thoroughly wash your hands, cooking equipment, and countertops before cooking, and be mindful when working with ingredients like raw meat and eggs.

When Packaging and Gifting

- When packaging the food, continue to be hygienic, and when transporting, monitor the temperature outside to ensure the freshness is never compromised.
- If the dish is not going to be eaten immediately upon gifting, include a note or label that has the date the dish was made, any instructions on heating, storing, etc., and its shelf life.

Preparing Japanese-Style Rice

Washing

The first and most integral step in preparing Japanese-style rice is to wash it. After measuring out the amount you wish to cook, pour it into a pot or large bowl, cover with water, and swish the grains back and forth with your hands; don't be too forceful while doing this, or you'll risk breaking the grains. When the water becomes milky*, drain it with a sieve and add fresh water. Repeat this process 3 or 4 times, until the water is mostly clear (it doesn't need to be 100%). Sieve the rice and let rest for 30 minutes.

Cooking

Place the rice in either a rice cooker or a heavy-bottomed pot or pan with a lid. One part rice to one part water is considered the standard proportion; after you've added the water, let the rice soak for 30 minutes (the older and drier the rice, the longer you should let it soak). If you're using a rice cooker, just turn it on; if you're using a pot, let the rice come to a boil over medium heat, then reduce to low, placing the lid on top. Cook for 10 minutes before taking off the heat, then let the rice sit for an additional 10 minutes. Fluff with a rice paddle and serve.

Making Sushi Rice

There are two recipes in this book—Congratulatory Sushi (page 74) and Good Luck Inarizushi (page 118)—that call for and detail how to make sushi rice. Fanning the rice as you add the *awase-zu*, or seasoned rice vinegar, is a very important step, as it prevents the rice from becoming mushy. Traditionally, this requires a hand fan (namely, a wide *uchiwa*-type fan), but alternatively, you could use an electric fan or even a hair dryer on the coolest setting. Once the seasoned rice vinegar is incorporated, you can stop fanning.

*In Japan, it is believed that washing your face with the milky rice water makes your skin softer.

Birthday Chicken Nuggets

Chicken nuggets are a perennial favorite for children and adults alike. And with the addition of tofu and vegetables, this recipe is nutritious and delicious. Adorn each nugget with a colorful homemade flag pick, and you have the perfect finger food to take to a children's birthday party.

Chicken Nuggets Recipe

Ingredients

- ¼ lb, or 4 oz, (100 g) firm tofu
- 1 medium-sized carrot
- 4 string beans
- 1 tbsp (15 ml) whole-wheat flour, plus additional for dusting
- ½ tsp (2.5 ml) salt
- White pepper, to taste
- 1 tsp (5 ml) soy sauce
- ¾ lb, or 12 oz, (340 g) ground chicken
- Canola oil, for frying
- Condiments (ketchup, lemon, barbecue sauce, etc.), for dipping

Directions (makes 15 to 20 pieces)

1. Wrap the tofu block in a paper towel and press softly to soak up excess liquid.
2. Finely chop the carrot and string beans. *Note: Try to cut the carrot as thinly as possible. If the pieces end up a little too thick, heat in a microwave until they become slightly soft, then add them to the mix in step 4, after they've cooled.*
3. Combine the whole-wheat flour, salt, white pepper, and soy sauce in a bowl or in a resealable freezer bag. *Note: If you prefer not getting your hands dirty when combining the mixture in step 4, knead the mixture through the plastic bag.*
4. Add the tofu, ground chicken, and vegetables to the mixture and knead thoroughly, breaking the tofu up with your fingers.
5. When thoroughly combined, form mixture into spoon-sized balls.
6. After dusting the nuggets on both sides in whole-wheat flour, fry in the canola oil for about 3 minutes on each side.

🍴 Tasty Tips

• When forming the mixture into nuggets, dribble a little canola oil onto your palms to make the task much less messy.

• Customize this recipe by adding different vegetables, herbs and spices, or even cheese.

🎁 When Giving as a Gift

Double-sided Tape   *Colored Paper*

Twist

• To make the flag picks, cut construction or wrapping paper into fun flag shapes and attach them to bamboo skewers or toothpicks with double-sided tape. Remember to work with clean hands, as the skewers will eventually be placed in the chicken nuggets. Either place the skewers into the nuggets before serving or have the children do it themselves.

• I recommend placing freshly fried nuggets in a basket lined with paper towels. Lightly cover them with some plastic wrap, then wrap the basket in a furoshiki (see page 151) for easy carrying. Place the sauces and condiments in mini-containers and toss them into the basket, too.

Chummy Potato Salad

I think you'll agree that it's more fun cooking for others than just for yourself, or why else would you be reading this book? But the real payoff is when you get to eat with the recipient of your little gift! While this potato salad recipe is on the simpler side, scooping it onto ice-cream cones tied with ribbons gives it a party-like presentation that's sure to make your feelings of friendship speak loud and clear.

Potato Salad Recipe

Ingredients

- 2 medium-to-large potatoes
- 1 small cucumber
- ½ tsp (2.5 ml) salt, plus additional
- ½ red onion
- 2 slices of ham
- ¼ cup (60 g) mayonnaise
- 1 tsp (5 ml) vinegar
- White pepper, to taste
- 6 small ice-cream cones

Directions (makes 6 cones)

1. Boil the potatoes, skins on, for 30 minutes, or until soft. Remove the skins.
2. Slice the cucumber, then quarter each slice. Sprinkle salt (in addition to the ½ tsp, or 2.5 ml, listed in the ingredients) and thoroughly massage it into the pieces. *Note: The salt helps sweat out any excess liquid.*
3. Chop the onion and dice the ham into ¼" (6 mm) cubes.
4. Place the potatoes in a bowl while still hot, then add mayonnaise, vinegar, ½ teaspoon (2.5 ml) salt, and white pepper. Mash well with a fork.
5. When the potato mixture has cooled, wring the excess water from the cucumber pieces with a paper towel and add to the mixture, along with the onion and ham. Combine thoroughly.
6. Use a spoon or, better yet, an ice-cream scoop, to scoop the potato salad onto the ice-cream cones.

♔ Tasty Tips

Add flavorings as you mash!

• The potatoes mash easier and absorb flavor better when still hot. So add flavorings as you mash!

• Play the role of an ice-cream scooper by scooping to order multi-colored potato salads. Add beets to the recipe to make it red, replace the potatoes with yellow squash for a golden tone, or add edamame for a green hue. Top with nuts and dried fruit!

⊞ When Giving as a Gift

• The easiest way to transport this dish is to place the potato salad in a container, carrying the ice-cream cones and scoop separately. That way you can have fun not only eating it together but also assembling it!

Wrap gently so as not to upset the potato salad!

• If you prefer scooping the potato salad onto the cones before transporting, gently cover each cone with plastic wrap and fasten with a ribbon or plastic tie near the top of the cone. Pack them gingerly into a basket or bag, standing them upright and preventing as little movement as possible during transportation.

• It's best to prepare the cones as close to eating as possible, or they will get soggy.

Good Impression Minestrone Soup

When preparing a home-cooked meal for a friend or loved one, naturally, you want to impress! But rather than tackling some complicated recipe, make this minestrone soup that's as impressive as it is easy to make. If you prefer to go that extra mile, use dried beans instead of canned beans, reconstituting them yourself. Prepare the beans a day before you make the soup, and the soup a day before you plan to eat it—despite the extra work, you'll be rewarded with a much deeper and delicious flavor.

Minestrone Soup Recipe

Ingredients

- ¼ cup (50 g) dried cannellini, or white kidney, beans
- 1½ tsp (2.5 ml) salt, divided (plus additional for flavoring)
- Black pepper, to taste
- 1 tbsp (15 ml) olive oil, plus additional for flavoring
- 1 medium-sized carrot
- ½ celery stalk
- ½ onion
- 2 tomatoes
- 1 garlic clove
- ½ lb (200 g) chicken
- 1 tbsp (15 ml) white wine
- 1 tsp (5 ml) cornstarch
- 1¼ cups (300 ml) water
- White pepper, to taste
- 1 tbsp (15 ml) mirin
- Fresh basil, to taste

Directions (makes 2 to 4 servings)

1. The day-before prep: Soak the beans in water overnight until they become plump and thoroughly reconstituted. Drain.
2. To cook: Fill a pot with plenty of water (separate from the 1¼ cups, or 300 ml, listed in the ingredients) and add a dash of salt and black pepper, olive oil, and the beans, simmering until the beans are soft. Let the beans cool in the liquid.
3. Chop the carrot, celery, onion, and tomatoes into pieces roughly the size of the beans. Crush or finely chop the garlic.
4. Cut the chicken into bite-sized pieces and dress in ½ teaspoon (2.5 ml) salt, white wine, and cornstarch.
5. Add the tablespoon (15 ml) olive oil and garlic to a different pot, and heat on low. When the garlic becomes fragrant, bring the flame up to medium and add the onion, carrot, celery, and 1 teaspoon (5 ml) salt, cooking until the onion turns translucent.
6. Add the water, tomatoes, white pepper, and mirin, and simmer for 30 minutes. *Note: If the liquid evaporates midway through, add another 1¼ cups (300 ml).* Once vegetables are soft, add the beans and chicken, and simmer, while skimming the scum.
7. When the chicken has cooked through, adjust the salt and black pepper to taste.
8. Just before serving, coarsely chop the basil and sprinkle over the soup.

🍴 Tasty Tips

• Whenever I am reconstituting dried beans, I tend to make extra; once rehydrated, I put them, along with the liquid they stewed in, into freezer bags and place in the freezer—this way, I always have some beans conveniently handy to use in soups and stews!

• If you're short on time, it's perfectly fine to use canned beans. You could also try using different beans, such as chickpeas or red kidney, or combine all three to make a nice mix.

Tossing the meat in cornstarch will also help result in a more tender texture.

• Adding the uncooked chicken last results in perfectly soft meat, even when using breast meat.

🎁 When Giving as a Gift

• When transporting, pour into a lidded plastic container or a large freezer bag. When you make it to the recipient's home, borrow a pot to heat it back up in.

• Wet the fresh basil and gently wrap in a paper towel before placing into a separate container—this will preserve the aroma for the recipient to enjoy when adding to the soup.

• You could also gift a bag of rice or a box of pasta, especially if you make enough soup for leftovers. Then the recipient can add the rice or pasta to the minestrone when eating it the next day.

Try rice…

…or pasta.

Neighborly Steamed Buns

There's nothing quite like a warm meat bun—called *baozi*, or *bao*, in Chinese—to fill you with energy. This goes double for homemade ones! The secret here is to use sliced meat instead of ground meat—it makes a big difference taste-wise! If you have a friend who lives nearby, arrange to run these up to her freshly steamed.

Steamed Buns Recipe

Ingredients

- ¾ cup (100 g) all-purpose flour, plus additional for dusting
- ½ tsp (2.5 ml) dry yeast
- ½ tbsp (7.5 ml) sugar
- Salt, to taste
- ¼ cup (60 ml) lukewarm water (about 100°F, or 40°C)
- ½ tbsp (7.5 ml) canola oil
- ⅛ lb, or 2 oz, (60 g) pork belly
- ¼ leek
- 2 shiitake mushrooms
- ½ tsp (2.5 ml) sake
- ½ tbsp (7.5 ml) oyster sauce
- ½ tbsp (7.5 ml) sesame oil
- Condiments (mustard, soy sauce, etc.), for dipping

Directions (makes 4 buns)

1. Combine the flour, dry yeast, sugar, and salt in a bowl. Add half the water and stir thoroughly, adding more water, depending on how dry or wet the dough becomes. Once everything is incorporated, add the canola oil and continue to knead the dough.
2. When the dough is soft and smooth, place a cloth over it, letting it rest in a warm place until it rises.
3. Cut the pork belly into ¼"-thick (6 mm) slices, and dice the leek and shiitake mushrooms. Dress the meat and vegetables in the sake, oyster sauce, and sesame oil.
4. When the dough has risen to twice its original size, sprinkle with flour and place on a cutting board. *Note: Be careful not to use too much flour or the dough will lose its stickiness, making it difficult to wrap the filling later.* Divide dough into 4 pieces, then roll out each piece into a flat circle about 4" (10 cm) in diameter. *Note: Leave the center a little thicker than the edges, as this will keep the filling from falling out.*
5. Spoon the filling onto the center of each of the dough circles. Making small pleats along the edges with your fingers, gather up the sides of the dough toward the center, then give them a good pinch to close the bun tightly. Repeat with the rest of the buns. Place each bun on parchment paper cut into 4" (10 cm) squares.
6. Wet the bamboo steamer with a little water and place the buns on their parchment paper inside of it. Leave them to rise for 10 minutes with the lid on so they don't dry out. Bring a pot of water to boil. Place the steamer on top of the pot of boiling water and leave for another 15 minutes with the lid on, until the buns finish steaming.

🍴 Tasty Tips

• Add some black sesame seeds to the dough for a fragrant flavor and interesting texture, or add curry powder to the filling for a spicier bun. You could also make pizza buns by adding dried basil to the dough and using cheese and tomato sauce as the filling. For a sweeter option, try *anko* (red bean paste) as a filling. The possibilities are endless!

🎁 When Giving as a Gift

• If the buns have cooled, lightly wet them with water, then wrap each one separately in a moist paper towel. Reheat for 30 seconds each in a microwave, and they will come out as fluffy as if just steamed.

Wrap separately and heat in the microwave.

• If you don't have far to go, I recommend just carrying them in the bamboo steamer; it's the perfect insulator for them. You could also gift the bamboo steamer along with the buns!

Happy Hour Antipasto

Lay out one or both of these light antipasti when spending the evening with friends, and you'll feel as if you're sitting in a special cafe. With a loaf of sliced baguette and some wine— or herbal tea, if you prefer—take your time catching up, chatting relaxedly late into the night.

Antipasto Recipes

Ingredients

Mushroom Garlic Sauté
- ½ pack (50 g) shimeji mushrooms
- ½ pack (100 g) enoki mushrooms
- 2 shiitake mushrooms
- 2 eringi mushrooms
- 2 garlic cloves
- 3 tbsp (45 ml) olive oil
- 1 tsp (5 ml) cumin seeds
- ½ tsp (2.5 ml) salt
- Black pepper, to taste

Semidry Tomatoes in Anchovy Oil
- 20 cherry tomatoes
- Salt, to taste
- 20 green olives
- 6 anchovy fillets
- Olive oil, to taste

Directions

Mushroom Garlic Sauté (makes 4 servings)
1. Slice the mushrooms; halve the garlic cloves and slice thinly.
2. Cook garlic in the olive oil on low heat. Once the garlic has browned, remove from pan and set aside for later.
3. Add the cumin seeds to the pan and continue cooking on low heat. *Note: If the olive oil dissipates, add more.* When the cumin seeds begin to bubble, raise the heat to medium-high, add the mushrooms, and sprinkle in the salt and pepper; then proceed to cook as if meaning to scorch it, moving the pan as little as possible. Once the mushrooms have cooked through, place the garlic back into the pan and combine well.

Semidry Tomatoes in Anchovy Oil (makes 4 servings)
1. Remove any stems from the tomatoes and halve them. Place them seed side down on paper towels, leaving for 10 minutes, to absorb excess liquid.
2. Lay out a sheet of aluminum foil in a baking pan and arrange the tomatoes seed side down. Sprinkle salt over them, then cook in the oven for 90 minutes at 250°F (120°C) to dry them out. Take out to drain, or wipe away, any excess fluids, then cook for another 30 minutes. *Note: Keep an eye on the temperature and time as you dry the tomatoes. When the liquid from the seed section has mostly evaporated and the skins are wrinkly, they're done.*
3. Halve the olives and roughly chop the anchovy fillets, then combine them with the tomatoes. Pour in enough olive oil to just cover.

🍴 Tasty Tips

• You'll find that drying the cherry tomatoes condenses their flavor and makes them sweeter. If you have the extra time, let them dry in the sun for half a day before cooking them in the oven; then they won't need to cook as long.

• If you don't have time to dry the tomatoes in the oven, you could always use store-bought sun-dried tomatoes.

• If there's leftover oil remaining in the tin or bottle that held the anchovies, add it in for a stronger anchovy flavor.

🎁 When Giving as a Gift

It's also convenient to have dishes (with lids) in varying sizes.

• If you bring these antipasti to a party or potluck, make little signs (see photo, pages 26–27) that describe what they are.

• Trays that have lids are great for transporting this dish, plus you can use them to serve the food in.

• Whenever I host a potluck party, I like to assign roles to avoid overlap. I give my guests a basic idea of what I'm making, so they can bring an item that complements my menu. Then, it's a nice surprise on the day of the party!

I'll bring the wine!

I'll bring some bread!

I'll bring dessert!

Party Pork Loin

When hosting a cocktail party, I recommend serving this dish, as it makes for a nice and filling hors d'oeuvre. The excitement in the room will be palpable as you cut the pork loin into hearty pieces before your guests. You can also use the leftover liquid in which the pork simmered to make a savory vegetable soup— that's two recipes in one, and sure to convince anyone of your cooking prowess!

Pork Loin & Vegetable Soup Recipes

Ingredients

Pork Loin
- 1 lb (500 g) pork loin
- 1 tbsp (15 ml) salt
- 1 garlic clove
- ½ cup (120 ml) white wine
- 1 bay leaf
- Water, as needed

Vegetable Soup
- 1 onion
- 2 medium-sized carrots
- 2 medium-sized potatoes
- 1 pack (100 g) shimeji mushrooms
- 1 sprig of thyme
- Salt, to taste
- Black pepper, to taste

Directions

Pork Loin (makes 4 servings)
1. The day-before prep: Wrap the pork loin, all around, with a piece of twine, then rub in the salt. Either place the loin on a plate covered in plastic wrap or in a resealable freezer bag, and leave in the fridge for an entire day.
2. To cook: Place the meat into a pot with plenty of water. Let it come to a boil, while carefully skimming the scum.
3. Add the garlic clove, white wine, and bay leaf. Lower the heat to medium and let simmer for 30 minutes. Add more water, if necessary.
4. Stab the loin with a bamboo skewer. If no red liquid comes out, it's done. Turn off the heat and let cool in the liquid.

Vegetable Soup (makes 2 to 4 servings)
1. Chop the onion into 8 wedges, cut the carrot and potato into roughly mouth-sized pieces, and remove the stems from the shimeji mushrooms and tear the caps into pieces with your hands.
2. Add the vegetables and sprig of thyme to the liquid the pork loin has been simmering in. *Note: If there's not enough liquid left, add some water.* Simmer for 20 to 30 minutes on medium heat. Once the vegetables have softened, add salt and pepper to taste. *Note: Be mindful of the amount of liquid versus salt in the soup and flavor accordingly.*

Tasty Tips

Twine...

...salt...

...ready to cook!

- If you don't have time to let the pork loin rest in the refrigerator for a day—although it really does make a big difference flavor-wise—try to let it rest for at least an hour.

- This soup is simply flavored with salt, but you can toss in some canned tomatoes to make it minestrone-like, or even add some soy sauce for an Asian flair. Feel free to customize the recipe to your own tastes, using seasonal vegetables for variety all year long.

What flavor shall I make it this time?

When Giving as a Gift

- When gifting, you can either slice the pork loin before you transport it or you can slice it with the recipient just before eating. It's up to you!

It makes a nice hors d'oeuvre by itself, or you can enjoy on top of bread or rice for a heartier option.

- Don't forget to include condiments! I personally enjoy grainy mustard, rock salt, and ponzu sauce with this dish.

Heartwarming Lasagna

There's nothing more comforting than the smell of cheese from a lasagna as it cooks. And the delicious taste can bring you up even when you're feeling down. If you have a friend who's feeling blue, bring her this dish. You'll both find that you'll be too busy blowing on hot forkfuls of the lasagna to bother dwelling on her sorrows.

Lasagna Recipe

Ingredients

Meat Sauce

- ½ onion
- 1 garlic clove
- 1 tbsp (15 ml) olive oil
- ½ lb, or 8 oz, (225 g) mix of ground beef and ground pork
- 1 tsp (5 ml) salt
- Black pepper, to taste
- Dash of allspice
- 2 tbsp (30 ml) red wine, optional
- ¾ cup, or 7 oz, (200 g) tomato purée

Béchamel Sauce

- 1 tbsp (15 ml) butter
- 2 tbsp (30 ml) all-purpose flour
- ½ tsp (2.5 ml) salt
- Black pepper, to taste
- ¾ cup (180 ml) milk

- 6 to 8 no-boil lasagna sheets
- Parmesan cheese, to taste

Directions (makes 2 to 4 servings)

1. Preheat the oven to 350°F (170°C).
2. To prepare the meat sauce: Chop the onion and garlic finely, and cook in the olive oil over medium heat. Once the onion turns translucent, add the ground meat, salt, pepper, and allspice, and cook until the meat becomes brown and crumbly. Add the red wine and tomato purée, and boil down for 5 minutes.
3. To prepare the béchamel sauce: Place the butter in a large microwavable bowl and cook for 1 minute. Add flour, salt, and pepper to the butter, then add the milk, little by little, whisking thoroughly as you do. Place back in the microwave and cook for 2 minutes, before taking out to whisk again. Then heat again for another 30 seconds, whisk, cook for 1 minute more, and then whisk a final time. Once the mixture thickens, the sauce is complete. *Note: Do take care to keep the mixture from bubbling over and to avoid contact with it as you take the bowl in and out of the microwave, since it will be very hot.*
4. Dip 2 lasagna sheets in water. In a small baking dish, place the lasagna sheets, then top with the meat sauce, followed by the white sauce. Repeat this 3 to 4 times, then cover the top with freshly grated Parmesan cheese.
5. Bake for 30 to 40 minutes, or until the top has browned.

🍴 Tasty Tips

• The delicious simplicity of this lasagna recipe is what makes it so great; however, if you would like to add more depth to the flavor, add some finely chopped mushrooms and celery to the meat sauce. Or add chili, cumin, and cardamom powders, along with kidney beans, to give it some spice.

• Feel free to add more vegetables (either on top or between the layers). Eggplant, okra, squash, cabbage, peppers... The options are endless! For denser vegetables, cook them in advance.

Try a mix of okra and eggplant as a topping!

• In this recipe, I use no-boil lasagna sheets, but if you prefer using the type that do need to be cooked first, follow the instructions on the box.

🎁 When Giving as a Gift

Prepare this dish in an aluminum foil pan; it's light and easy to carry, plus there's no dishwashing when done!

• If you are unable to deliver the lasagna fresh out of the oven, make sure to tell your friend to enjoy it when piping hot. You could even include a little card with heating instructions!

Movie Night Popcorn

All of your friends are gathered to watch a movie, so, naturally, the snack you have prepared is that classic: popcorn. Make one spicy and one sweet, and there will be no end to the grabbing hands. Just be sure to make a lot so it lasts through the movie!

Popcorn Recipes

Ingredients

Crispy Caramel
- ¼ cup (50 g) popcorn kernels
- 2½ tbsp (37.5 ml) butter, divided
- ¼ tsp (1.25 ml) salt
- ⅓ cup (65 g) sugar
- 1 tbsp (15 ml) water

Prickly Chili Pepper
- ¼ cup (50 g) popcorn kernels
- 2 tbsp (30 ml) olive oil, divided
- ¼ tsp (1.25 ml) salt
- 1 tsp (5 ml) chili powder

Directions

Crispy Caramel (makes 4 servings)
1. Combine the popcorn kernels, ½ tablespoon (7.5 ml) butter, and salt in a pan with a lid. Cover and cook over high heat, occasionally shaking the pan.
2. After about 2 minutes, the kernels should begin to pop. Shake the pan continuously. *Note: If you do not, the popcorn will burn.* Once the number of pops you hear lessens, turn off the heat and remove the lid, or the steam will make the popcorn mushy.
3. Add the sugar, 2 tablespoons (30 ml) butter, and water to another pan and cook over high heat. Mix occasionally by shaking the pan to and fro. *Note: If you mix with a spatula, the sugar will crystallize and become granular, so refrain from doing this.* Once it has turned a nice caramel color, turn off the heat.
4. Add the popcorn to the caramel and quickly mix to to coat evenly. *Note: Even after you've turned off the stove, the residual heat may cause the caramel to burn, so try to do this fast. Also, be careful not to burn yourself with the hot caramel.* Lay out a sheet of parchment paper and spread the caramel covered popcorn on it to prevent it from sticking together as it cools.

Prickly Chili Pepper (makes 4 servings)
1. To cook the popcorn, follow steps 1 and 2 in the Crispy Caramel recipe, exchanging the butter for 1 tablespoon (15 ml) olive oil.
2. Combine the chili powder with the remaining tablespoon (15 ml) of olive oil, then pour over the popcorn, making sure it is well coated. Mix well.

♙♥ Tasty Tips

Freshly made and oh-so crunchy!

• The darker the caramel gets— before it burns, of course—the more bitter and mature the flavor will become. For salted caramel popcorn, increase the amount of salt in the recipe.

• If you want to make a spicy popcorn with something other than chili powder, try curry or wasabi powder, butter and black pepper, or sesame oil and shichimi spice. These spicy popcorns pair well with beer or sake.

Mixing the oil with the seasoning first makes it much easier to evenly coat the popcorn.

🎁 When Giving as a Gift

• If packed into containers while still warm, the popcorn will end up moist due to the steam. So wait until it has thoroughly cooled first.

• For transporting, pack the popcorn in cardboard take-out boxes, then carry them in a furoshiki (see page 151). Also bring spoons for scooping and enough paper cups to hold everyone's portions.

Summer Barbecue Fish

When you are invited to the customary summer barbecue and want to grill something other than hot dogs and hamburgers, fish is the name of the game. Taking the time to marinate the fish the day before in herbs and garlic will result in a truly great taste. This dish goes great with beer, and the most popular way to eat this dish in Japan is on top of rice with a squeeze of lemon and a splash of soy sauce.

Fish Recipe

Ingredients

- 4 whole horse mackerel
- 2 twigs of rosemary
- 1 garlic clove
- ⅓ cup (80 ml) olive oil
- 1 tsp (5 ml) salt
- Black pepper, to taste
- Assorted vegetables
    (eggplant, okra,
    peppers, etc.), optional
- Cooked rice, optional
- Lemon, optional
- Soy sauce, optional

Directions (makes 4 servings)

1. The day-before prep: Remove the guts, hard fin near the tail on both sides, and the scales (if they still have them) from the mackerel. Clean under cold running water, then wrap in a paper towel to soak up the excess moisture. Slice the garlic clove.

2. Fill the mackerel's stomach with the rosemary twigs and the sliced garlic clove.

3. Place the fish and olive oil in a resealable freezer bag. Press out all excess air and zip shut, allowing the fish to soak overnight in the refrigerator.

4. To cook: Remove the fish from the plastic bag and season with the salt and pepper. Grill, along with any vegetables you've prepared, until both sides of the fish are roasted a golden brown. *Note: This recipe assumes you are cooking on an outdoor grill, but the fish can be prepared in the same way when cooking indoors with a frying pan.*

5. If eating on top of rice, add a squeeze of lemon and a splash of soy sauce before digging in.

🍴 Tasty Tips

• You can use the same cooking method with fish fillets, shrimp, and even chicken. When working with poultry, rub a little salt in before soaking to help the meat become thoroughly marinated.

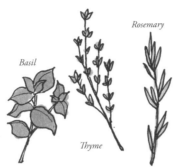

Rosemary

Basil

Thyme

• Other herbs you could use to season the fish are thyme, dill, oregano, parsley, and basil.

🎁 When Giving as a Gift

• If you don't have time to let the fish soak overnight, at least let it marinate in a freezer bag while you travel to your destination.

Carry in a cooler to ensure freshness.

Great Outdoors French Toast

Everything seems more delicious when you eat it outdoors on a nice day, especially your favorite foods! This French toast is made with thickly sliced baguette, and by letting the bread soak for a time in the eggs and milk, you will find that the end result is incredibly soft and light. And why not make your own butter, too? The taste of fresh butter is out of this world.

French Toast & Homemade Butter Recipes

Ingredients

French Toast
- 4 1"-thick (2.5 cm) slices of French baguette
- 2 eggs
- 1 cup (240 ml) milk
- ¼ cup (50 g) sugar
- Drizzle of olive oil
- Honey, to taste

Add honey to taste.

Homemade Butter
- ¾ cup (180 ml) cream
- ½ tsp (2.5 ml) salt

Directions

French Toast (makes 2 servings)
1. Place the baguette slices into a resealable freezer bag. Whisk the eggs, milk, and sugar together, then pour into the bag. Push out all excess air and zip shut. Leave in the fridge, shaking occasionally, for at least an hour or up to half a day.
2. Heat the olive oil in a frying pan or hot plate, then add the bread slices. *Note: If there is any extra liquid remaining in the plastic bag, pour on top of the bread.* Put a lid over the pan and let cook until the middle has cooked through. *Note: If the heat is too strong, the surface of the bread will burn while the inside remains uncooked, so be careful.* Cook each side for about 3 minutes. *Note: If the bread bounces back up after you press down on it with your finger, it's done.*
3. Top with honey and homemade butter.

Homemade Butter
1. Pour the cream and salt into a disposable plastic bottle, tightly seal the cap, and begin shaking up and down vigorously. After about 10 minutes, it will stop making sloshing sounds, but continue shaking well.
2. After about 20 minutes of shaking, the butter will have come together. Good job!
3. Open the cap and pour out the excess liquid (whey). Cut the bottle in half with a serrated knife, and enjoy on the French toast.

♟ Tasty Tips

• Try adding vanilla bean or vanilla extract to the egg mix for a richer flavor.

If you cut the vanilla bean lengthwise, it's easier to scoop out the seeds inside with a knife. I recommend using a vanilla bean that's at least 1" (2.5 cm) long.

• You could also add freshly ground pepper and herbs to the homemade butter to make it more savory.

• Did you know that the leftover liquid from making butter, called whey, is high in nutrients? So feel free to drink it, if you'd like!

🎁 When Giving as a Gift

• To save some time, let the bread soak up the egg mixture while you're transporting it to your destination. Then, it will be ready to cook when you arrive!

Yay!

• Since the butter-making process can be a little tiring, pass the bottle around to the people in your group, with everyone taking a turn shaking the bottle—doing this will prove to be fun and rewarding for both children and adults.

Have the Day Off Fruit Punch

You don't have to resign yourself to feeling stressed. On your days off from work, make time to head out for a picnic—but don't even think about talking about your job! You bring this refreshing fruit punch, while your friends bring the great conversation. With glass in hand, smell the scent of fresh grass carried by the breeze, and feel your frustrations being carried away, too.

Fruit Punch Recipe

Ingredients

- 1¼ cups (300 ml) water
- 1½ cups (150 g) sugar
- 1 star anise
- 1¼ cups (300 ml) white wine
- Assorted fruit (strawberries, kiwis, pineapple, blueberries, etc.)
- 8 bamboo skewers

Directions (makes 4 servings)

1. Put the water, sugar, and star anise into a pot and bring to a boil, then let simmer for 3 minutes.
2. Turn off the flame, add the white wine, and let cool.
3. Cut the fruit into bite-sized pieces.
4. Skewer the fruit pieces onto the bamboo skewers.
   Note: Alternate the placement of fruit on the skewer for a colorful, attractive look.
5. Once the punch has completely cooled, pour into a bottle and add the fruit.

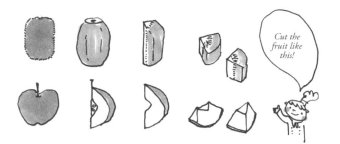

Cut the fruit like this!

🍴 Tasty Tips

Cherries, grapes, apples, watermelon...

• For best results, use fruit that is in season. In spring and summer, include grapefruit, plums, cherries, melon, and watermelon; in autumn and winter, include bananas, figs, persimmons, pears, apples, and kumquats.

• You could also enjoy the fruit soaked in the punch, like a sangria.

• I prefer sweeter wines, but a drier one works, too. For a tarter flavor, add a little lemon juice to the mixture.

🎁 When Giving as a Gift

• The use of skewers makes it easier to enjoy the fruit. I suggest using 8 in the recipe, but depending on the size of the bottle, you can use more or less. Just remember that the skewers should fit inside as tightly as possible to keep the fruit from jostling around too much; since fruit is sensitive and easily bruised, take care while transporting.

• Don't forget to bring the glasses!

Picnic Potato Chips

When you're on a picnic, enjoying the surrounding nature, surely you want a nice natural flavor to go with it. These homemade potato chips deliver just that! Frying interesting root vegetables, such as lotus root and *gobo* (burdock root), along with the trademark potato, turns this recipe into a healthy snack with an addictive flavor. And for those with a sweet tooth, I have also included an easy recipe for creamy caramels.

Potato Chips & Creamy Caramels Recipes

Ingredients

Potato Chips

- ¹⁄₁₀ of a kabocha squash
- 2 medium-to-large potatoes
- 1 lotus root
- 1 small satsumaimo (Japanese sweet potato)
- 2 stalks of gobo (burdock root)
- Canola oil, for frying
- Salt, to taste

Creamy Caramels

- ⅓ cup (80 ml) milk
- ½ cup (100 g) sugar
- 1 tbsp (15 ml) honey
- ¾ cup (180 ml) cream

Directions

Potato Chips (makes 3 snack bags worth)

1. Slice the kabocha squash, potatoes, lotus root, and satsumaimo very thinly, about 1 mm thick. *Note: I recommend using a slicer for this, if you have one.* Soak everything, except the squash, in water. Peel thin strips off the gobo with a peeler.
2. Lay all the vegetable slices on paper towels and allow them to dry, preferably in the sun, for half a day.
3. Heat the canola oil and begin frying. *Note: If the temperature of the oil gets too hot, the chips will burn, so reduce the heat if it gets too high.*
4. Once fried, lay the chips atop paper towels to soak up any excess oil, and salt them while they're hot.

Creamy Caramels (makes 30 to 40 small pieces)

1. Place parchment paper in a small square-shaped baking pan and set aside.
2. Put the milk, sugar, and honey into a pot, stirring with a plastic spoon over low heat.
3. When the sugar has dissolved, add the cream, bring the heat up to low-medium, and simmer for 20 minutes, while continuously stirring. *Note: To ensure it doesn't burn, stir methodically, scraping upward from the bottom of the pan.*
4. When the color of the mixture becomes a nice light brown and is firm enough so you can no longer see the bottom of the pan when stirring, lower the heat.
5. Once it reaches the desired thickness, quickly pour into the prepared pan, let cool, and place in the refrigerator for an hour. *Note: Be careful not to burn yourself with the hot caramel.* Once it has firmed up, cut into pieces with a knife and wrap in cellophane.

🍴 Tasty Tips

- Though it may be a little time consuming, leaving the sliced vegetables out to dry before you fry them is really integral: it gets rid of the excess liquid in the vegetables, leading to a much crispier result.

- For salted caramels, add about ¼ teaspoon (1.25 ml) salt to the mix. Try adding nuts during the cooking process, too. It's delicious!

- Don't feel boxed in by the potato. Experiment with different vegetables for your chips!

🎁 When Giving as a Gift

- After the chips have cooled, place them into oil-proof gift bags. With the addition of a piece of yarn or ribbon as a handle, they're perfect for handing out to children.

If you don't have cellophane on hand, you could wrap in glassine paper or even some parchment paper.

Knot the ends of a piece of yarn or ribbon together.

Double-fold the top of the bag over the yarn, and staple in place.

- Individually wrap the caramels in festive multicolored cellophane.

- The caramels do melt easily, so try to keep them out of the sun as much as you can when taking outdoors.

Nourishing Ratatouille

Your busy friend is always eating takeout... Have you ever worried that he's not getting enough vegetables in his diet? If so, this nutrient-rich ratatouille is just the ticket. With this dish, he can look forward to the tender potatoes, fluffy turnips, and rich tomato sauce that is begging to be sopped up with a nice piece of crusty bread at the end of the meal.

Ratatouille Recipe

Ingredients

- 2 medium-sized carrots
- 4 satoimo (taro root)
- 1 lotus root
- ½ gobo (burdock root)
- ½ onion
- 1 turnip, with greens
- 1 garlic clove
- 1 tbsp (15 ml) olive oil
- 1 can, or 14 oz, (400 g) canned whole tomatoes
- 1 tsp (5 ml) salt, plus additional for flavoring
- White pepper, to taste
- 2 tbsp (30 ml) mirin
- 1 tsp (5 ml) soy sauce
- Black pepper, to taste

Directions (makes 2 to 4 servings)

1. Peel the carrot, satoimo, lotus root, and gobo, then coursely cut into bite-sized pieces.
2. Quarter the onion and cut the turnip into 6 wedges. Chop the turnip greens to about 1½" (4 cm) in length. Crush or finely chop the garlic.
3. Add olive oil and garlic to a pot and heat on low. Once the garlic becomes fragrant, add all of the vegetables, except for the turnip and its greens.
4. Stir in the canned tomatoes, 1 teaspoon (5 ml) salt, white pepper, and mirin, combining well. Place a lid on the pot and let simmer for 30 minutes over medium heat. Take care to stir occasionally to prevent it from burning.
5. When the satoimo has cooked through, add the turnip, turnip greens, and soy sauce. Put the lid back on and let simmer for 10 more minutes.
6. Add salt and black pepper, to taste. *Note: Allowing the ratatouille to cool a little before eating will let the flavors really commingle.*

🍴 Tasty Tips

Add your favorite type of sausage... They all go well!

• You could also try adding daikon radish, potatoes, sweet potatoes, or yamaimo. Or try different arrangements, depending on the season.

• And for someone who really won't be satisfied unless there's meat mixed in, bacon and sausage go well with this dish. Or perhaps a boiled egg or some delicious cheese? Customizing a recipe to the recipient's tastes is one of the best parts of making a little gift!

🎁 When Giving as a Gift

Also wrap up any bread, wine, and glasses in a nice cloth.

• When transporting, I suggest carrying the dish in an enamel pot with a lid. Though it's a little heavier, you don't have to worry about the tomato sauce staining the insides. Wrap it up in a furoshiki (see page 151), and you'll also have a nice little tablecloth!

Comforting Cabbage Potage

If you're planning an outdoor date when the weather is still a bit chilly, a big blanket and a thermos full of this potage are essentials. The comforting warmth and hearty consistency of this soup will ensure you have an enjoyable time. If preparing this recipe in the spring, use spring cabbage and new potatoes—this will result in an even more naturally sweet, light flavor.

Cabbage Potage Recipe

Ingredients

- ¼ cabbage head
- ½ medium-sized potato
- ½ tsp (2.5 ml) salt, plus additional for flavoring
- ½ cup (120 ml) water
- ⅔ cup (160 ml) milk
- 1 tsp (5 ml) butter
- White pepper, to taste

Directions (makes 2 to 4 servings)

1. Cut the cabbage into rectangles and its core into thin slices. Slice the potato.
2. Add the cabbage, potato, and ½ tsp (2.5 ml) salt to a pot with the water, and cook over medium heat.
3. Place a lid on the pot and let simmer for 15 to 20 minutes, or until the potatoes become fork tender and the cabbage is very soft. *Note: If the water dissipates too quickly, add more in small amounts for a steaming—as opposed to a boiling—effect.*
4. Pour from the pot into a blender, pulsing on and off, until the mixture becomes paste-like. Add the milk, while keeping an eye on the consistency. *Note: You don't want the consistency to become watery when adding the milk.*
5. Return to the pot to reheat, adding the butter, as well as the white pepper and salt, to taste. Heat to just before boiling, then take off the flame. *Note: Be careful not to let the potage boil when reheating.*

Tasty Tips

• Adding onion to the potage will result in a milder flavor. For another variation, add some curry powder to the vegetables, while they are stewing, or substitute soy milk for regular milk. I do recommend keeping the butter, though, for the rich finish it gives.

When Giving as a Gift

• Carry the potage in a thermos with a wide mouth. Before pouring the soup into the thermos, fill it with hot water—doing this will not only sanitize the thermos but also raise the temperature inside.

• And don't forget the bowls, spoons, and a loaf of crusty bread!

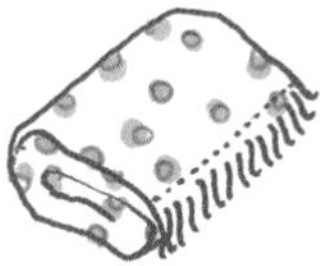

Bring a blanket for warmth and towels for clean up.

Teatime Scones

If you're planning teatime with a friend on a nice sunny day, why not make your theme "Anne of Green Gables"? The sweet and tart scent of the jam as it cooks and the fragrance of freshly baked scones will raise your spirits as much as the lovely weather. And because they are a gift to a friend as dear as Anne's friend Diana, take care in arranging them artfully in a quaint wicker basket.

Scones and Jam Recipes

Ingredients

Scones
- ¾ cup (100 g) cake flour
- 1 tbsp (15 ml) sugar
- ¼ tsp (1.25 ml) salt
- 1 tsp (5 ml) baking powder
- 2 tbsp (30 g) butter
- ¼ cup (60 ml) milk
- Flour, for dusting

Strawberry Jam
- 1 pint, or 2 cups, (300 g) small-sized strawberries
- ⅓ cup (65 g) sugar
- 1 tsp (5 ml) lemon juice

Yuzu Marmalade
- 3 yuzu
- 2⅛ cups (500 ml) water
- ½ cup (100 g) sugar

Directions

Scones (makes 6 small scones)
1. Preheat the oven to 400°F (200°C).
2. Combine the cake flour, sugar, salt, and baking powder in a food processor. Dice the butter into ½" (13 mm) cubes, add to the food processor, and pulse.
3. When the mixture becomes crumbly, add milk and pulse again, until it becomes a big lump. Place on a flour-dusted board and roll dough to 1¼" (3 cm) thickness. Cut into circles and bake for 15 minutes.

Strawberry Jam (makes 2 small jars worth)
1. Remove stems from strawberries, clean, and pat dry. Place into a pot, add sugar, and leave for 30 minutes.
2. Drain any excess liquid from the pot and bring to a simmer on high heat, until it reaches your desired consistency. Stir in the lemon juice, then take off the heat. Spoon into a jar, screw on the lid, and let cool.

Yuzu Marmalade (makes 2 small jars worth)
1. Clean and halve the yuzu. Scoop out the flesh, inner membrane, and seeds and place in a pot. Set the peels aside. Pour in water and let come to a boil, while skimming the scum. Lower the heat and let simmer for 30 minutes. When half the liquid has cooked down, sieve it, pressing down firmly on the yuzu flesh with a wooden spoon. Set the liquid aside.
2. Thinly slice the peels, then repeat the simmering/sieving process from step 1, saving the peels and not the liquid this time.
3. Simmer the liquid from step 1 and the peels from step 2 together, occasionally stirring, for 20 minutes. When the peels turn soft, add the sugar and simmer for another 20 minutes, then take off the heat. Spoon into a jar, screw on the lid, and let cool.

🍴 Tasty Tips

- There are two secrets to getting strawberry jam to the perfect consistency: The first is to use strawberries that are on the smaller side. The second is to not cook it for too long! While taking care that it doesn't burn, cook quickly over high heat.

- This strawberry jam has less sugar than usual, resulting in a slightly shorter shelf life. So be sure to refrigerate and eat up as soon as possible.

- If yuzu are unavailable, oranges, lemons, and grapefruits can be used, too!

- Enjoy the yuzu marmalade mixed in hot water for yuzu tea.

- Did you know that the seeds and inner membrane of the yuzu contain pectin, the essential component for thickening jam?

🎁 When Giving as a Gift

Be sure to sterilize the jars in boiling water before use.

- Try to make the scones the same width as the small jars of jam, wrapping them on top of each other in clear plastic for a little gift.

- If you plan on eating the scones soon after gifting them, also provide a spoon for easy scooping of the jam.

End of the Week Sangria

Cheers to making it through another week! And there's nothing better to toast with than this sangria, which has dried fig juice as its base. Catching up with a friend as you slice cheese for a cheese plate, I'm sure you'll find that although you prepared this sangria for someone else, it's a well-deserved gift for you, too.

Sangria Recipe

Ingredients

- ⅓ cup (50 g) dried figs (the large, soft type)
- 1¾ (400 ml) sweet red wine
- 1 cinnamon stick
- 1¾ (400 ml) orange juice

Directions (makes 4 servings)

1. Remove any hard stems that may be on the dried figs, then cut into slices about ½" (13 mm) thick.
2. Place the figs, ½ cup (120 ml) red wine, and the cinnamon stick in a microwavable bowl covered with plastic wrap, and heat in the microwave for 2 minutes, or until the figs become soft. Let steam for 5 minutes before removing the plastic wrap, then allow to cool. *Note: If you're in a hurry, you can speed up the cooling process by sitting the bowl in ice water.*
3. Once it has cooled, remove the cinnamon stick and set it aside for later. Pour the mixture into a blender, add another ½ cup (120 ml) wine, and blend. Once the figs become paste-like, add the rest of the wine and the orange juice, mixing everything lightly together. *Note: When blending, keep an eye on the amount of wine you're using, adding little by little. The sangria should have a paste-like consistency that's not too watery and not too thick.*
4. Pour the mixture into a clean bottle and add back in the cinnamon stick.

♟ Tasty Tips

• In lieu of orange juice, cut an orange into round slices. You could also soak the orange slices in wine for a day or two prior to adding to the mix.

• If you prefer a slightly tarter flavor, substitute the orange juice with grapefruit juice.

When Giving as a Gift

If you don't have a lid for your bottle, just put plastic wrap over the top and secure it with a rubber band.

If your bottle has a cork or a cap, remember to twist it on tightly!

• Since this sangria is to be a special treat for you and your friend, try bringing real glasses with stems, instead of disposable ones. Add some ice in a cooler, and you're all set!

Congratulatory Sushi

For a celebratory party, it's worth putting in a little more effort to make an impression. And this colorful, bite-sized sushi dish perfectly fits the bill. With four varieties—light white-fleshed sea bream, boiled shrimp, smoked salmon, and even ham for those who don't like fish—everyone is sure to find something to enjoy.

Sushi Recipe

Ingredients

- 3 tablespoons (45 ml) rice vinegar
- 2 tablespoons (25 g) sugar
- 2 teaspoons (10 ml) salt
- 1½ cups (300 g) Japanese rice
- 1 2"-sheet (5 cm) of kombu (kelp)
- 4 boiled shrimp
- 8 slices of sea bream sashimi (sliced thinly)
- 4 slices of smoked salmon
- 4 slices of ham
- Salmon roe, fresh dill, mayonnaise, radish or pea sprouts, white sesame seeds, lemon, etc., for toppings
- Soy sauce, for dipping

Directions (makes 16 pieces)

1. The day-before prep: Mix the vinegar, sugar, and salt together to make the *awase-zu*, or seasoned rice vinegar, leaving overnight in the fridge. *Note: Doing this will increase the depth of flavor.*
2. To cook: Wash the rice thoroughly (see page 9) and place in a rice cooker with an equal amount of water (1½ cups, or 320 ml), and cook with the sheet of kombu over it.
3. Once it's cooked, add the seasoned rice vinegar and, with a fan blowing wind onto the rice (see page 9), mix gently while turning the rice over so that it doesn't become mushy. To prevent it from drying out, cover with a wet cloth and let cool.
4. Butterfly the boiled shrimp; slice the lemon, then quarter the slices; and cut the sprouts short.
5. In the center of some plastic wrap, place 2 slices of the sea bream sashimi and about 2½ to 3½ tablespoons (30 to 40 g) sushi rice on top of the fish. Lift the 4 corners of the wrap and shape the sushi into a round shape by gathering and then twisting the corners together (see illustration, opposite). Remove the plastic wrap and top with salmon roe.
6. Repeat step 5 with the rest of the sea bream slices, as well as the other ingredients. Top the shrimp with the lemon, the salmon with the dill and mayo, and the ham with the sprouts and sesame seeds.

♨ Tasty Tips

Fish->Rice->Lift, Gather, and Twist->Open->Topping->Eat!

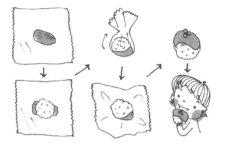

• Feel free to vary the choice of toppings, depending on the party guests' tastes.

• I did not include wasabi in the recipe so that children can enjoy this dish, too, but you could certainly incorporate some for the adults.

🎁 When Giving as a Gift

• Either line up sushi of the same type in rows to make stripes or mix them up for a colorful collage. Be creative with your presentation!

• Try to prepare this dish as close to the start of the party as possible. While transporting it, take care that conditions are right so that the fish doesn't lose its freshness en route, particularly in the warmer seasons.

Take extra special care while making and transporting the sushi so that the ingredients remain hygienic.

Rewarding Roast Beef

Here's the perfect dish to bring to a party celebrating your hard-working, meat-loving friend. Arrange the roast beef on a showy platter with fresh, colorful vegetables, and it will look like the party has been catered by a professional. And there's no need to use your oven; all you need is a frying pan and some aluminum foil. This is one party main you will want to make a regular part of your culinary repertoire.

Roast Beef Recipe

Ingredients

- 2 1-lb (500 g) blocks of round steak
- 2 tsp (10 ml) salt
- Ground black pepper, to taste
- 2 garlic cloves
- 2 tbsp (30 ml) olive oil
- ½ cup (120 ml) red wine
- 1 tbsp (15 ml) soy sauce
- 1 tbsp (15 ml) lemon juice
- Vegetables (green leaf lettuce, radicchio, asparagus, turnips, cherry tomatoes, lemon, etc.), optional

Directions (makes 6 to 8 servings)

1. Let the cut of meat come to room temperature after taking it out of the refrigerator. *Note: It should reach room temperature after about an hour.* Rub in the salt and pepper thoroughly.

2. Finely chop or crush the garlic cloves. Cook the garlic in the olive oil on low heat. When the garlic becomes fragrant, remove the garlic from the pan and set it aside for later.

3. Place the meat in the same pan on high heat and cook each side for 2 to 3 minutes. Once both sides have cooked, pour in the red wine and add back the garlic. Let simmer for 5 minutes on low heat. Turn the meat over once and let simmer for another 5 minutes. Check the doneness by stabbing the meat with a bamboo skewer; if no red liquid comes out and the skewer is warm to the touch, the meat is cooked through. *Note: Depending on the thickness of the cut and/or how you prefer your beef cooked, you may need to cook longer.*

4. Remove the meat from the pan and, while it's hot, wrap securely in aluminum foil and let rest for 30 minutes. Once it's completely cooled, begin slicing.

5. For the dipping sauce: Using the same pan you cooked the meat in, add the soy sauce, lemon juice, and any meat juice from the aluminum foil. Combine and let it come to a quick boil. *Note: Depending on the amount of meat juice left, be mindful of the amounts of soy sauce and lemon juice you add.*

6. On a platter of your choosing, place the roast beef atop a bed of green leaf lettuce and radicchio, before arranging the rest of the vegetables around the meat.

🍴 Tasty Tips

• Use different vegetables, depending on the season. Just make sure to incorporate lots of different colors for an eye-catching presentation.

For a sandwich, a thicker bread pairs well.

• For this recipe, I've utilized the fresh flavor of soy sauce mixed with lemon for the dipping sauce, but you could also add grated garlic to it, or do a simple horseradish or wasabi mix. You could even mix with grainy mustard. They're all great choices!

Preparing a variety of dipping sauces for a different taste with each bite is a fun idea.

• To make this into a meal unto itself, you could either serve the meat in sandwiches or on top of rice.

🎁 When Giving as a Gift

• To prevent the meat from drying out while transporting, securely wrap it in plastic wrap and carry with a cooling pack.

• I recommend serving this dish on an aluminum tray, as it will invoke the image of having been catered by a professional.

The ever-useful furoshiki!

• If you don't have a bag big enough to carry everything, then don't forget your furoshiki (see page 151)!

Fresh Start Plum Wine

Japanese plums, or *ume*, are considered lucky and are a great gift for those making a fresh start. This plum wine is shockingly easy to make, and once you've finished the initial preparation, all you have to do is wait for the distillation process to work its magic. Soon enough, you'll discover that this delicious wine will prove to be an excellent gift to give, year after year.

Plum Wine Recipe

Ingredients

Made with Unripened Green Ume

- 2¼ lbs (1 kg) unripened green ume plums
- 3 cups (700 ml) orange blossom honey
- ½ tsp (2.5 ml) brandy

Made with Fully Ripened Ume

- 2¼ lbs (1 kg) fully ripened ume plums
- 3 cups (700 ml) lotus honey
- ½ tsp (2.5 ml) white liquor

Directions (makes 4 liters)

1. Prepare 4 separate 1-liter containers. Wash them in hot water, then let dry. Label the containers with the date.
2. Wash the plums in water, taking care not to bruise them. Remove any stems. With a dry cloth, wipe the plums dry, one by one. *Note: Use a cloth that will not leave behind cotton residue.*
3. Place the plums, honey, and alcohol into the containers.
4. Leave the containers in a cool spot, away from direct sunlight. Gently shake the bottles up and down 1 to 2 or times a day until the honey dissolves entirely.
5. The wine will be ready to drink after just 3 months, but allowing it to mature longer will make the flavor much smoother and nice. *Note: I like to wait 6 months to a year.*

Tasty Tips

Try different combinations for a variety of flavors.

Making your own wine allows you to understand and enjoy the distillation proecess.

• I prefer using honey, but you could also use white or brown sugar lumps; likewise, you could use rum or even whiskey as your spirit.

• Unripe green plums usually begin arriving at Japanese groceries from May to June, so get them while they're in-season.

•In order to keep the plum wine fresh for as long as possible, use a spirit with an alcohol percentage of 35 or higher.

When Giving as a Gift

Cutting the fabric with pinking shears gives it a decorative edge and prevents it from unraveling.

• When gifting, pour the wine into smaller bottles. Since the plums are also delicious, as well as visually inviting, add a few to each bottle.

• With a pair of pinking shears, cut out a circular cloth a little larger than your lid, then tie it around the lid with a ribbon for a festive look.

• If you have room in your bag, bring along some soda water to make and enjoy plum wine-flavored spritzers.

Best Wishes Marble Cakes

These bite-sized white cakes, marbled with bittersweet raspberries, are an ideal match for engagement parties and bridal showers. When decorated with symbols of happiness or good luck, like a bow or four-leaf clover, and arranged in an elegant box, you'll be amazed by their transformation into a fancy-looking gift.

Marble Cakes Recipe

Ingredients

Marble Cakes
- 7 tbsp (100 g) unsalted butter
- 2 eggs
- ¼ cup (60 g) frozen raspberries
- ½ cup (100 g) sugar
- ¾ cup (100 g) cake flour
- 1 tsp (5 ml) baking powder

Syrup
- 1 tbsp (15 ml) rum
- 1 tbsp (15 ml) honey

Icing
- ¼ cup (50 g) sugar
- 2 tsp (10 g) egg whites
- Pink and white dragées, optional

Directions (makes a small baking pan worth)

1. Let the butter and eggs come to room temperature; defrost the raspberries, then mash them with a fork; preheat the oven to 325°F (170°C); and lay parchment paper in the baking pan.
2. Stir the butter until it's creamy, then add the sugar and beat until soft and white.
3. Whisk the eggs, then add them, little by little, to the butter and sugar, while mixing. *Note: If you add the eggs all in one go, the mixture won't incorporate.*
4. Combine the flour and baking powder, then add in 2 parts to the mixture from step 3, stirring in with a plastic spatula. *Note: Incorporate the first part of the flour mixture well before adding the second part.*
5. Place a quarter of the batter into a separate bowl, then mix in the raspberries. Pour the batter with raspberries back into the main bowl of batter and stir widely and loosely to create a marble pattern. *Note: If you mix too thoroughly, you'll lose the marbling effect.*
6. Pour batter into the baking pan and bake for 35 to 40 minutes. For the syrup, combine the rum and honey and, after removing the cake from the oven, quickly coat with the syrup while it's hot. Once the cake has cooled, cut into bite-sized squares.
7. To make the icing: Whisk, or beat, the sugar and egg whites together. *Note: If it becomes too soft, add more sugar; too hard, add more egg whites.* Decorate with bow and clover designs, then top with the dragées.

♟ Tasty Tips

- You could also bake these cakes in a pound cake pan.

You will be delicious…

You will be delicious…

Make your own icing bag using a plastic bag or a cone made from parchment paper.

con

gra

tu

lati

ons

- When decorating with the icing, don't feel limited to bows and clovers. Try writing the recipient's name or even a message!

🎁 When Giving as a Gift

- If you want to give these marble cakes an especially fancy touch, place them in an elegant wooden box. If you don't have one, then a simple cardboard box lined with origami paper is a good substitute. To prevent the cakes from drying out, make sure the box has a lid that fits firmly.

Choose paper with a celebratory design.

Long-Lived Red Bean Rice

This healthy and celebratory red bean rice dish is a traditional Japanese meal and the perfect gift for a health-conscious friend. The super-nutrious mix of assorted grains that are chock-full of minerals, along with some pickled vegetables, will speak of how much you respect your friend's choice of lifestyle.

Red Bean Rice & Pickled Vegetables Recipes

Ingredients

Red Bean Rice
- ⅓ cup (70 g) black-eyed peas
- 2⅛ cups (500 ml) water
- ¾ cup (150 g) Japanese white rice
- 1½ cups (300 g) mochi rice
- ⅓ cup (65 g) mix of assorted grains

Pickled Vegetables
- 1 medium-sized carrot
- ¼ daikon radish
- Salt, to taste
- 1 tbsp (15 ml) vinegar
- ½ tsp (5 ml) sugar

Directions

Red Bean Rice (makes 4 servings)
1. Rinse the black-eyed peas, then place them in a pot with just enough water to cover them and bring to a boil. Drain the peas.
2. Bring 2⅛ cups (500 ml) water to a boil. Add the black-eyed peas, lower the heat, and let simmer for 10 minutes, while skimming the scum. *Note: The peas will also cook in a rice cooker in step 4, so they only need to reach a halfway level of softness.* Turn off the heat. Once cool, remove the beans, while saving the liquid they have cooked in for later use.
3. Combine the Japanese white rice and mochi rice and wash thoroughly (see page 9). Put the rice into a rice cooker and add a 2¾ cups (650 ml) combination of all the cooking liquid from step 2 and water. Add the black-eyed peas and mixed grains, then turn on the switch.
4. After it's finished cooking, let steam for 15 minutes, then gently mix everything together before serving.

Pickled Vegetables (makes 2 servings)
1. Slice the carrot and daikon, cut into flower shapes, and dust with a little salt to sweat out excess liquid. Wring out the excess water with a paper towel.
2. Dress with the vinegar, sugar, and a dash of salt. Once it's absorbed, the vegetables are ready to eat.

⚑ Tasty Tips

Black-eyed peas

Red beans

- Black-eyed peas and red adzuki beans may seem similar, but they are actually from two different legume species. Black-eyed peas are traditionally used in red bean rice because their color comes off on the rice more easily, giving the dish its red color. Also, their husks are thicker and not as fragile, making them easy to mix in with the rice.

- In the winter, try using yuzu juice instead of vinegar for the pickles; or in summer, add some finely chopped myoga to the mix. Either way is delicious!

Whatever you add, strive for cohesion in taste.

🎁 When Giving as a Gift

- Try packing the rice in a simple round wappa (Japanese wooden box) for a classic Japanese feel. But don't pack the rice too tightly, or it will be hard to scoop out once it's cooled.

- For a nice touch, include chopsticks with custom wrapping made of origami paper. You could even write a message on the paper!

Game Night Fried Fish Cakes

Add a Japanese twist to your game night menu with these fried fish cakes that are not only deeply rich in flavor but are also a staple in traditional Japanese homes. They go especially well with sake and beer. This recipe calls for *gobo* (burdock root) and edamame, but no matter what vegetables you choose to incorporate, everyone will enjoy the variety of tastes, colors, and textures.

Fried Fish Cakes Recipe

Ingredients

- ¼ gobo (burdock root)
- ½ medium-sized carrot
- ⅓ lb (150 g) cod
- ⅓ lb (150 g) shrimp
- ¼ lb, or 4 oz, (100 g) firm tofu
- 1 egg
- 1 tsp (5 ml) soy sauce
- 1 tsp (5 ml) sugar
- 1 tbsp (15 ml) mirin
- ¼ tsp (1.25 ml) salt
- ½ cup (75 g) boiled edamame
- Vegetable oil, for frying
- Soy sauce, for dipping

Directions (makes 15 to 21 cakes, 3 different types)

1. Cut the gobo and carrot into short slivers. *Note: If you cut into larger pieces, parboil beforehand.*
2. Cut the cod into bite-sized pieces; peel and devein the shrimp, then cut into thirds. Wrap the tofu block in a paper towel and press softly to soak up excess liquid.
3. Put the cod, shrimp, tofu, egg, soy sauce, sugar, mirin, and salt into a food processor and blend until smooth.
4. Take the mixture from the food processor and divide into 3 bowls, mixing in one of each of the following 3 ingredients into each of the bowls: gobo, boiled edamame, and carrot.
5. Divide the 3 mixtures into 5 to 7 cakes each and mold them into your preferred shapes. *Note: In the photo on pages 94–95, I formed the gobo cakes into an oval, the edamame cakes into a long, narrow shape, and the carrot cakes into a little ball.*
6. Fry the cakes in vegetable oil, while occasionally flipping, for 4 to 5 minutes.

♟️ Tasty Tips

• Before starting the cooking process, prepare all necessary utensils and ingredients, and cook quickly so that the freshness of the seafood never becomes compromised. Take special care that your hands don't warm up the fish cakes while forming them into shapes, and place any unused portions into the refrigerator immediately.

It doesn't matter if they come out misshapen...as long as they're made with love!

• When forming the mixture into shapes, dribble a little vegetable oil onto your palms to make the task much less messy.

🎁 When Giving as a Gift

You can also put them into a freezer bag and then into the basket.

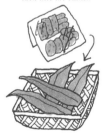

• When transporting, lay out banana leaves in a basket and place the fish cakes on top. If they're still hot, cover with paper napkins. Then, tie the whole thing up with a furoshiki (see page 151).

• If the fish cakes have cooled, or you are going to be taking them a long way, then wrap tightly in plastic wrap and carry them in a cooler.

• Re-heat the cakes in a toaster oven or on a grill. They're delicious when eaten cold, too.

Cooking them over an open flame creates an appetizing aroma.

Dorayaki Gathering

When your whole family is gathered together, hold a dorayaki-making party to liven up the afternoon! Laying out the pancakes separate from the fillings allows for easy customization and will delight both the children—who can enjoy these with a tall glass of milk—and the adults—who can pair with coffee or tea. This recipe is inspired by my mother, who loves sweet red bean paste and who always complains that there's too little found in the store-bought versions.

Dorayaki & Red Bean Paste Recipes

Ingredients

Dorayaki Pancakes
- 2 eggs
- 1 tbsp (15 ml) honey
- ⅓ cup (65 g) sugar
- ¾ cup (100 g) cake flour
- 1 tsp (5 ml) baking powder
- 1 tbsp (15 ml) water

Red Bean Paste
- 1 cup (200 g) red adzuki beans
- 1 cup (200 g) cane sugar

Whipped Cream
- ½ cup (120 ml) heavy whipping cream
- 1 tablespoon (15 ml) sugar

Directions

Dorayaki Pancakes (makes 24 pancakes, or 12 pairs)
1. Whisk the eggs, honey, and sugar together until the mixture becomes thick and foamy. Combine the cake flour and baking powder, then add to the egg mixture. *Note: Mix lightly to prevent it from becoming gummy.* Cover the bowl with plastic wrap and let sit at room temperature for 30 minutes.
2. Stir in the water, checking that the batter is at a good consistency. *Note: If it's too thick, it will be difficult to form small pancakes; add more water if necessary.*
3. Place the pan on low heat, and spoon out the batter, 1 tablespoon (15 ml) at a time, in circles. Cook for 2 minutes, or until the the batter begins bubbling, then flip and cook for 1 minute.
4. Cover pancakes with a cloth and let cool.

Red Bean Paste
1. Rinse the red beans. Place in a pan, cover with water, and cook on high heat for about 10 minutes. Drain.
2. Return beans to the pot, fill with enough water to cover them and let come to a boil. Lower the heat and let simmer for an hour, while skimming any scum. *Note: If the water dissipates, add more; there should always be enough water to cover the beans.*
3. When the beans are soft enough to squash between your fingers, drain any excess water and add the sugar in 3 parts, stirring up from the bottom of the pan to make sure it doesn't burn. Allow to boil down. Once it thickens, it's ready.

♟ Tasty Tips

Enjoy as a family!

• Try adding a little powdered green tea to the dorayaki batter for a nice color and slightly bitter taste.

• Sandwich bananas and strawberries between the cakes, along with the filling and whipped cream.

• You could also add ground black sesame seeds to the red bean paste for another version of the filling.

🎁 When Giving as a Gift

For the whipped cream, place the sugar and cream in a bowl, and whisk, or beat, vigorously until it peaks!

• If you don't have far to travel, line a small basket with plastic wrap or parchment paper and place the pancakes, along with a container of the red bean paste, inside. To prevent the pancakes from drying out, wrap them tightly in plastic wrap. Carry the basket in a furoshiki (see page 151). If you have farther to go, pack the dorayaki and filling in plastic containers with lids.

Freshly made dorayaki is delicious!

• It might be easiest to bring the ingredients for the whipped cream and make it fresh at your destination.

Housewarming Brandy Cake

If you're planning a visit to your in-laws and want to bring them something that's homemade and impressive, I recommend trying your hand at this brandy cake recipe— which tastes its best three days after it's been made. Though it's a little extra work to make it in advance, it will be well worth the effort when you taste how smoothly the rich flavors of the butter and brandy blend with the tartness of the apricots.

Brandy Cake Recipe

Ingredients

- 7 (tbsp) 100 g unsalted butter
- 2 eggs
- 1 cup, or 4 oz, (120 g) dried apricots
- ⅔ cup (160 ml) brandy, plus additional
- ½ cup (100 g) sugar
- ⅔ cup (90 g) cake flour
- 1½ tbsp (20 g) almond powder
- ½ tsp (2.5 ml) baking powder
- ½ cup (100 g) sugar

Directions (makes a 6", or 16 cm, round mold worth)

1. Let the butter and eggs come to room temperature and preheat the oven to 325°F (170°C).
2. Place the dried apricots and ⅔ cup (160 ml) brandy in a microwavable bowl, cover in plastic wrap, and cook for 2 minutes in a microwave. Once it's cooled, halve 3 apricots that have retained their shape—for decoration—and set them aside. Finely chop the rest of the apricots. Set aside the brandy that wasn't absorbed by the apricots for later use.
3. Stir the butter until it's creamy, then add the sugar and beat until soft and white. Whisk the eggs, then add them, little by little, to the butter and sugar, while mixing. *Note: If you add the eggs all in one go, the mixture won't incorporate.*
4. Combine the flour and almond and baking powders, then add in 2 parts to the mixture from step 3, stirring in with a plastic spatula. *Note: Incorporate the first part of the flour mixture well before adding the second part.* Add the chopped apricots and 3 tablespoons (45 ml) leftover brandy. *Note: Mix lightly to prevent the batter from becoming overworked.*
5. Pour the batter into the mold, arrange the decorative apricots on top, and bake for 35 to 40 minutes. After taking it out of the oven and, while it's still hot, coat the top with any remaining brandy. *Note: If there's none or very little left, use new.*
6. Remove from the mold and let cool, then coat again with brandy. Wrap in plastic wrap, place in refrigerator, and coat with brandy each day prior to eating.

⚔ Tasty Tips

Try dried fruit steeped in alcohol.

• Instead of apricots, use raisins, dried blueberries, or any other dried fruit you prefer.

• Dried fruit steeped in alcohol will result in a deeper flavor.

• Add some chopped nuts, too! Roasting the nuts first will result in a more fragrant cake.

Spread out the nuts in a baking pan. You could also cook in a frying pan.

🎁 When Giving as a Gift

• For this recipe, I used a regular round cake mold, but you could also bake in a loaf pan or even as madeleines, for smaller gifts. When cooking as madeleines, shorten the baking time to between 20 and 25 minutes, and keep a sharp eye on them to ensure they don't burn.

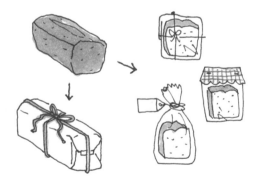

Tailgate Kebabs

What's the first food you think of when attending a sporting event? In Japan, it's definitely these kebabs, or *kushikatsu*. Here, I share recipes for two kinds of kebabs: meat and omelet. And so that you can comfortably eat them while cheering on your favorite team, these kebabs are conveniently bite-sized and placed on a stick.

Kebabs Recipes

Ingredients

Meat Kebab

- ⅓ lb (150 g) pork loin
- Salt, to taste
- Black pepper, to taste
- 1 to 2 eggs
- Flour, for dusting
- 1 cup (100 g) panko, for coating
- Vegetable oil, for frying
- Tonkatsu sauce, for dipping

Omelet Kebab

- 2 eggs
- ¼ cup (60 ml) dashi broth
- 1 tsp (5 ml) sugar
- Salt, to taste
- Vegetable oil, as needed
- Tonkatsu sauce, for dipping

Directions

Meat Kebab (makes 6 kebabs)

1. Thinly slice the pork loin into 6 slices, then lay the slices on a cutting board. Season with the salt and pepper, and roll them up (see illustration, opposite). *Note: Tuck in the sides to create a nice even shape.*
2. Whisk the egg(s) in a bowl. Dust both sides of the pork loin slices in flour, dip in the egg, and coat with the panko.
3. Fry the meat kebabs in vegetable oil for 3 to 4 minutes each.

Omelet Kebab (makes 6 kebabs)

1. Whisk the eggs, broth, sugar, and salt together.
2. Grease a pan with a paper towel dipped in vegetable oil, then place on high heat. Once the pan is hot, pour in half the egg mixture and spread it around so that it coats the entire pan.
3. When the bottom of the egg mixture has cooked but the top remains half uncooked, begin rolling it up. Roll it to the side of the pan, lightly grease the empty spaces of the pan with the oil-dipped towel, then pour in the remainder of the egg mixture and repeat the process, rolling the already rolled egg within the new egg. *Note: You may want to watch an online video to see the rolling technique (see Resources, page 149).*
4. Place the rolled omelet onto a cutting board and, once it's cooled, cut into 6 pieces. Stick on a bamboo skewer along with a meat kebab.

♈ Tasty Tips

• When rolling up the slices of meat for the meat kebabs, try sandwiching a shiso leaf, some cheese, or nori seaweed inside for an interesting flavor.

• For the omelet kebab, chopped leeks and carrots (parboiled beforehand) make for a delicious addition, too.

Other options include...

...lettuce...

...almonds...

...sour plums...

...and even marmalade!

• If you have trouble rolling your omelette while it's in the pan, wrap it in aluminum foil or a sushi mat while it's still hot. Use your hands to set the shape and, as it cools, it will take on that shape.

As long as it's still soft, it's easy to change the shape.

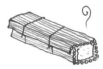

🎁 When Giving as a Gift

Sticking a toothpick in each piece makes for easier eating!

• If making a lot of kebabs for a big party, then pack them in a box and stick with individual toothpicks, in lieu of skewers, for easier sharing and eating.

• These also make great hors d'oeuvres.

Place the tonkatsu sauce in containers with lids.

Energizing Honey-Lemon Drink

Did you know that the citric acid in lemons has a great effect on relieving tiredness? That's why this honey-lemon drink mix is the perfect thing to bring to picnics and sporting events in the summer, adding soda water to it for a cool refresher. You can also enjoy it in winter, mixed with hot water to warm you up from the inside out.

Honey-Lemon Drink Recipe

Ingredients

- 2 lemons
- ¼ cup (70 ml) honey
- Soda water, as needed
- Apple mint, optional

Directions (makes 4 servings)

1. Wash and dry the lemons. *Note: Since you will also be able to eat the lemons and their peels, I recommend using either organic lemons or washing them very thoroughly beforehand.*
2. Remove the seeds and cut the lemons into very thin slices, with the peels still on. *Note: The thinner they're sliced, the easier they'll be to eat.*
3. Place the slices into a bowl, add the honey, and mix well. Place in the refrigerator.
4. Leave for about a day, after which the honey and lemon will have become fully incorporated.
5. Scoop a little of the mixture into a cup, add soda water, and drink (and eat).
6. If you like, muddle in some apple mint for an extra kick.

🍴 Tasty Tips

Remove the seeds and slice as thinly as possible

• Aside from drinking, this honey-lemon mix also tastes delicious when spread on toast or on top of ice cream.

• The mix will keep in the refrigerator for about a week.

🎁 When Giving as a Gift

• When taking outdoors, place the drink mix into individual cups with a little apple mint, then cover them with plastic wrap held in place by a rubber band. You could also pour the mixture into a jam jar, so everyone can spoon out the mix at their own convenience.

• If presenting as a gift, bring along a bottle of soda water and a muddler, so the recipient can drink up whenever she pleases.

In a Pinch Mini-Sandwiches

During times when your child might be too nervous to eat—perhaps it's the day of a piano recital—these emergency mini-sandwiches should do the trick. Because of their small size, they're filling without making one feel stuffed. And in addition to the standard savory, I've included sweeter sandwiches made with squash and cream cheese. Wrap a box in paper of your choosing, and you've got a custom sandwich carrier.

Mini-Sandwiches Recipes

Ingredients

- 8 slices of sandwich bread

Egg and Cucumber
- 2 hard-boiled eggs
- 1 tbsp (15 g) mayonnaise
- Salt and pepper, to taste
- ½ cucumber

Tuna and Tomato
- 1 can (150 g) tuna
- 2½ tbsp (38 g) mayonnaise
- Salt and pepper, to taste
- 2 small-sized tomatoes

Kabocha Squash
- ¾ cup (100 g) kabocha squash
- 1 tbsp (15 g) mayonnaise
- Salt and pepper, to taste
- 1 to 2 lettuce leaves

Ham and Cream Cheese
- ⅓ cup (80 g) cream cheese
- 1 tsp (5 ml) maple syrup
- 2 slices of ham

Directions (makes 16 mini-sandwiches)

1. Remove the bread crusts, construct the sandwiches, and quarter each one when cutting.

Egg and Cucumber
1. Separate the whites and yolks of the eggs. Finely chop the whites and place them with the yolks in a bowl. Mash well, adding mayonnaise, salt, and pepper.
2. Slice the cucumber thinly, for laying on top of filling.

Tuna and Tomato
1. Drain excess liquid from the tuna, place in a bowl, and mash well, adding mayonnaise, salt, and pepper.
2. Remove stems from the tomatoes and slice them. Place them on top of a paper towel to soak up the excess liquid, then layer on top of filling.

Kabocha Squash
1. Dice the squash into ½-inch (13 mm) cubes with the peel on. Place in a microwavable bowl, cover with plastic wrap, and cook for 3 minutes in a microwave. Once soft, mash well, adding mayonnaise, salt, and pepper.
2. Wash and dry the lettuce, then layer on top of filling.

Ham and Cream Cheese
1. Let the cream cheese soften before adding the maple syrup. Mix together well.
2. Layer ham on top of the cream cheese.

🍴 Tasty Tips

• When cutting the sandwiches, hold the bread gently in place with the hand that's not holding the knife, then move the knife back and forth through the bread, without applying force. This technique will result in clean slices. Wrapping the sandwiches in plastic wrap as you cut will also keep the fillings in place.

Carefully move the knife back and forth firmly but without applying excess pressure.

• Prepare some paper towels that have been wetted to clean off the knife between slicing so as not the mix the fillings.

For a spicier flavor, add ssome mustard to the sandwich bread.

🎁 When Giving as a Gift

Put glue on the sides...

• If you wrap a somewhat shallow box in your favorite wrapping paper and lay down a piece of parchment paper inside, you've got a one-of-a-kind sandwich box.

• To prevent the sandwiches from drying out, wrap the entire box in plastic wrap. Don't forget the napkins!

...and cut the length of the paper at twice the heighth of the sides of the box.

Good Luck Inarizushi

According to Japanese legend, foxes are considered auspicious creatures with mystical powers, including shape-shifting. Their only weakness is fried tofu, or *aburage,* which makes inarizushi one of their favorite foods. The sweet and sour flavor of the fried tofu pouches goes perfectly with that of the vinegared sushi rice. Plus, it's a good vegetarian sushi option. Share this conveniently bite-sized dish backstage at a ballet or dance recital, and this lucky little treat is sure to assuage any cases of stage fright!

Inarizushi Recipe

Ingredients

- ¼ cup (60 ml) rice vinegar
- 4 tbsp (45 ml) sugar, divided
- 1 tsp (5 ml) salt
- 6 fried tofu pouches
- 2 tbsp (30 ml) soy sauce
- 4 tbsp (45 ml) sugar, divided
- 1 tbsp (15 ml) sake
- ⅔ cup (160 ml) water
- ½ medium-sized carrot
- ¼ gobo (burdock root)
- 2 shiitake mushrooms
- ¼ cup, or 1 oz, (30 g) bamboo shoots
- 6 snow peas
- 1¼ cups (250 g) Japanese white rice
- Radish or pea sprouts, optional

Directions (makes 12 pouches)

1. The day-before prep: Mix the vinegar, 1 tablespoon (15 ml) sugar, and salt together to make the *awase-zu*, or seasoned rice vinegar, leaving overnight in the fridge. *Note: Doing this will increase the depth of flavor.*

2. To cook: Place the fried tofu pouches between 2 paper towels and roll with a rolling pin to make them easier to open. Cut the pouches in half.

3. Combine the soy sauce, 3 tablespoons (45 ml) sugar, sake, and water in a pot and let come to a boil. Add the pouches, then cover with a lid. Lower the heat to medium and let simmer while occasionally stirring, until the liquid is completely absorbed by the pouches. *Note: When stirring, take care not to tear the pouches.*

4. Finely chop the carrot, gobo, mushrooms, and bamboo shoots; remove the stringy part from the snow peas and slice into short, thin strips.

5. Wash the rice thoroughly (see page 9) and place in a rice cooker with an equal amount of water (1¼ cups, or 300 ml). Place the carrot, gobo, mushrooms, and bamboo shoots on top and cook. Once it has cooked, add the snow peas, cover, and let steam for 15 minutes.

6. Add the seasoned rice vinegar and, with a fan blowing wind onto the rice (see page 9), mix gently while turning the rice over so that it doesn't become mushy. *Note: You will also be mixing the vegetables with the rice at this point.* To prevent it from drying out, cover with a wet cloth and let cool.

7. Form the rice into balls that fit inside the pouches and top with the sprouts.

🍴 Tasty Tips

You can vary the size depending on the occasion.

• To prevent the pouches from coming apart when cut in half, pack in just enough rice so that it's firm but not overly stuffed. If not cutting the pouches in half—for a normal-sized inarizushi—pack the rice in a little more gently.

• When forming the rice balls, wet your hands with vinegar. Not only will this keep grains of rice from sticking to your hands, but it will also act as an antiseptic.

Using vinegar on your hands instead of water will also keep the flavor from diluting.

🎁 When Giving as a Gift

• Wrap the inarizushi in a bamboo sheath and tie with a cute ribbon for an old-fashioned Japanese look. Then place in a plastic bag and carry in a furoshiki (see page 151).

• If you're bringing the dish backstage, pack several pairs of chopsticks and napkins for easy sharing.

Invigorating Ginger Syrup

When you want to prepare something tasty for a sick friend, this ginger syrup is easy to drink and may even help stir one's appetite. Add a spoonful or two to hot tea and, as the warming effect kicks in, your friend will be sure to feel the well wishes you have put into the syrup, too.

Ginger Syrup & Ginger Chips Recipes

Ingredients

Ginger Syrup

- ⅔ lb, or 3 cups, (300 g) ginger root
- 1 cup (200 g) sugar
- 1 bay leaf, halved
- 1 cinnamon stick, halved
- 5 cloves
- 1¼ cup (300 ml) water
- 1 tsp (5 ml) lemon juice

Ginger Chips

- Sugar, to taste

Directions

Ginger Syrup (makes about 1¾ cups, or 400 ml)

1. Remove the peel from the ginger, then slice very thinly, about 1 mm thick. *Note: I recommend using a slicer for this, if you have one.*
2. Place the ginger, sugar, bay leaf, cinnamon stick, and cloves into a pot, combine thoroughly, cover with a lid, and let sit for half a day. *Note: In the summer, let sit in the refrigerator instead.*
3. Once the ginger slices have sweated out their liquid, add the water, and cook over high heat.
4. When the mixture begins to boil, skim the scum and let simmer for 30 minutes.
5. Add the lemon juice, then take off the flame.
6. Strain the syrup into a bottle.

Ginger Chips

1. Leave the ginger slices (from step 6 above) to dry, preferably in the sun. Once they're semidry, coat in sugar.

Tasty Tips

• Mix the ginger syrup with hot tea, and you've got a warming drink, perfect for when you're sick; mix with soda water, and you've got ginger ale! Either way, the flavor will prove to be refreshing and not overly sweet.

• Besides enjoying as a drink, try it as a topping on plain yogurt or vanilla ice cream.

Blend with ice for a ginger shake!

When Giving as a Gift

Be sure to sanitize the bottles before pouring the syrup into them.

• Place a handwritten label with a personalized message on your bottle for an extra-special touch.

• When gifting the ginger chips, place them into a clear plastic bag or colorful gift bag, fold over the top, and staple a ribbon onto the flap. Finish by tying the ribbon into a bow.

Get well soon!

Thanks for every-thing!

Get Well Soon Flan Pudding

Doesn't everyone deserve to indulge in something delicious on occasion? Especially when feeling under the weather? Well, when you have a cold or sore throat, there's not much you *can* eat, so it's as good a time as any to dig into this special treat. Bring this flan pudding to a sick friend, and she's sure to start feeling better in no time.

Flan Pudding Recipe

Ingredients

Flan
- 3 whole eggs
- 1 egg yolk
- 1¼ cup (300 ml) milk
- ½ cup (100 g) sugar
- Sprinkling of vanilla bean

Caramel Sauce
- 1 cup (200 g) sugar
- ¼ cup (60 ml) water
- ⅓ cup (80 ml) hot water

Directions

Flan (makes a small glass baking dish worth)
1. Preheat oven to 350°F (180°C).
2. Gently whisk the 3 whole eggs and 1 egg yolk together, trying to avoid making air bubbles.
3. Place the milk, sugar, and vanilla bean into a small pot. Once it's heated to about 110°F (45°C), pour in the eggs, little by little, while whisking.
4. Sieve the mixture from step 3 into the glass baking dish, then place dish into a larger baking tray. Fill the tray with hot water (in addition to the ⅓ cup, or 80 ml, listed in the ingredients) and place in the oven. Let steam for 40 minutes, checking on it halfway through. *Note: If it seems about to burn, cover with foil.* Once it's finished cooking, turn off the heat and leave in oven for an additional 10 minutes.

Caramel Sauce
1. Put sugar and water into a pot and cook on medium heat. Shake the pot back and forth, every now and then, to evenly mix. *Note: Do not stir the mixture with a spatula, as doing this will result in the sugar crystalizing and becoming granular.*
2. Once it's a nice caramel brown color, take off the heat and quickly add the hot water. *Note: Take care that no hot sugar flies out of the pan and burns you.* Once it's settled, stir with a spatula and it's done.

🍴 Tasty Tips

• This is a standard recipe for Japanese-style flan pudding. The milk and egg provide plenty of nutrition, so it's an ideal food for when you're feeling sick.

Add as much caramel sauce as you'd like!

• You can decide how much or how little caramel sauce you'd like on your flan. The pudding is tasty by itself, too!

🎁 When Giving as a Gift

• Once the dish has cooled, neatly wrap plastic around your container and tie with a ribbon. Put the caramel sauce in a bottle with a lid. Place both items in a sturdy bag, or wrap in a furoshiki (see page 151) to transport. It will be a little heavy, so be careful since you're carrying glass!

Lift Your Spirits Bavarian Cream

I think we can all agree that eating is fun, but it's easy to forget that when you're recovering from an illness. So why not let this Bavarian cream remind you? This recipe uses brown rice, which is not only healthy but also results in a nice texture. Whether recovering at the hospital or at home, this is a dessert that will put anyone in a good mood.

Bavarian Cream Recipe

Ingredients

- 1 cup (240 ml) milk, divided
- 1½ tablespoons (10 g) powdered gelatin
- ¾ cup (150 g) cooked brown rice
- 4 egg yolks
- ⅓ cup (80 g) sugar, plus 2 tbsp (30 ml)
- 1 tbsp (15 ml) rum
- 1¼ cup (200 ml) cream
- Chervil, optional

Directions (makes 4 pudding cups worth)

1. Pour ⅔ cup (160 ml) milk into a small pot, sprinkle in the powdered gelatin, and let sit until it swells up.
2. Place the cooked rice and ⅓ cup (80 ml) milk into a food processor and blend into a still-lumpy paste.
3. Whisk the egg yolks and ⅓ cup (80 g) sugar together, until it becomes whitish in color, then add the rice paste from step 2 and the rum. Combine.
4. When the gelatin mixture from step 1 has swelled, cook over medium heat and stir until the gelatin completely dissolves. *Note: Don't let it come to a boil.* Add the mixture from step 3, little by little, combining thoroughly.
5. Once it's incorporated, rest the bowl inside another bowl full of ice water, letting it cool, while occasionally stirring, until it thickens.
6. In a different bowl, combine the cream and 2 tablespoons (30 ml) sugar, and whisk together for 6 minutes, or until it becomes thick enough that it peaks.
7. Add the mixture from step 4 to the mixture from step 6, in 2 or 3 increments, mixing well each time.
8. Rest this bowl inside the bowl full of ice water and stir until the mixture becomes slightly viscous. *Note: Stir gently so as not to collapse the bubbles in the cream.* Pour into cups and let chill in the refrigerator for at least an hour before serving. Garnish with chervil.

Tasty Tips

• You could also use white rice in this recipe, but the addition of brown rice results in a wonderful texture and adds a nice dose of fiber for a healthier treat.

• It's important to let the Bavarian cream firm up while you're stirring it in a bowl of ice water (see step 8, opposite)—doing this will ensure a soft but slippery bavarois that won't separate while in the refrigerator.

When Giving as a Gift

• You could serve the bavarois in either glass or plastic cups. Since the gelatin makes it quite firm, you could also slip it out of the cup and straight onto a plate. Garnish with some fresh fruit, and you've got a fancy-looking and delicious dessert.

Keep Up the Good Work Shortbread

To encourage your friend who's rushing to meet an important deadline at work, make these savory cheesy shortbreads for him. He can nibble on them at his desk or take them out to the park for a little break. But no matter where he eats them, he'll be sure to taste your support.

Shortbread Recipe

Ingredients

- ¾ cup (100 g) cake flour
- ½ cup (60 g) all-purpose flour
- 2 tablespoons (30 ml) sugar
- 1 teaspoon (5 ml) ground black pepper
- 7 tbsp (100 g) salted butter
- ½ cup (50 g) grated Parmesan cheese

Directions (makes 40 cookies)

1. Line a baking sheet with parchment paper and preheat the oven to 325°F (160°C).
2. Put the cake flour, all-purpose flour, sugar, and pepper into a food processor, and pulse until it's well incorporated.
3. Dice the butter into ½-inch (13 mm) cubes and add to the food processor, along with the Parmesan cheese. *Note: The butter should be chilled.* Pulse again.
4. Once the mixture becomes crumbly, transfer it into a large resealable freezer bag. *Note: Be careful not to overwork the dough in the food processor. If the crumbly dough sticks to your hand, it will result in that crispy yet soft texture that's signature of good shortbread.*
5. With either your hands or a rolling pin, shape the dough into a square about ½" (13 mm) thick. Let sit in the refrigerator for an hour. *Note: Make sure the plastic bag is sealed tightly to prevent the dough from drying out.*
6. Remove the dough from the plastic bag and cut it into roughly 1" (2.5 cm) squares with a kitchen knife. Arrange the pieces on the baking sheet and bake for 15 minutes.

🍴 Tasty Tips

- Instead of black pepper, you could add dried basil to the dough.

- Don't feel restrained by the square shape; try molding your shortbread into different shapes.

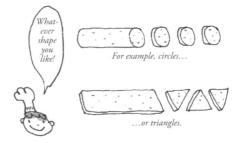

Whatever shape you like!

For example, circles...

...or triangles.

🎁 When Giving as a Gift

Good luck at work today!

- When gifting, try to reuse a cookie or cracker tin. Place a piece of parchment paper inside and layer the shortbread on top. If you don't have a tin, place in a plastic or brown paper bag and tie with a ribbon.

- Pair the shortbread with a pack of instant coffee to allow for a nice break, wherever or whenever.

Fortifying Banana Muffins

These banana muffins are the perfect fortifying treat for your friend who is studying for an important exam. She can easily eat a muffin with one hand, leaving the other hand free to tap at the computer or hold a book. And for as light and fluffy as they are, these banana muffins are jam-packed with nutrients to help keep her energy up and her mind sharp.

Banana Muffins Recipe

Ingredients

- 7 tbsp (100 g) unsalted butter
- 2 eggs
- 2 bananas
- 1 tsp (5 ml) lemon juice
- 1 tbsp (15 ml) grated ginger root
- ½ cup (100 g) sugar
- ¾ cup (100 g) cake flour
- 1 tsp (5 ml) baking powder
- ½ cup (100 g) sugar
- 1 tbsp (15 ml) rum
- 1 tbsp (15 ml) honey

Directions (makes 6 to 8 muffins)

1. Let the butter and eggs come to room temperature; preheat the oven to 325°F (170°C); and mash the bananas, lemon juice, and grated ginger together with a fork.

2. Stir the butter until it's creamy, then add the sugar and beat until soft and white. Whisk the eggs, then add them, little by little, to the butter and sugar, while mixing. *Note: If you add the eggs all in one go, the mixture won't incorporate.*

3. Combine the flour and baking powder, then add in 2 parts to the mixture from step 2, stirring in with a plastic spatula. *Note: Incorporate the first part of the flour mixture well before adding the second part.*

4. Add the banana mixture from step 1, mixing it in gently so as not to overwork the batter.

5. Pour batter into a greased muffin pan and bake for 35 to 40 minutes.

6. Combine the rum and honey, then coat the muffins with it as soon as you take them out of the oven.

🍴 Tasty Tips

• This is the perfect snack to eat when you're feeling tired. The sweet aroma of the vitamin-rich bananas is guaranteed to perk you right up.

• These muffins keep for about a week, and actually taste best when they're a couple days old. For this reason, I suggest making them in large batches.

Once the muffins have cooled...

...store them immediately so they don't get too dry.

🎁 When Giving as a Gift

• After baking the muffins, wrap them up in plastic bags with a tie or place them into individual boxes, like the ones in the photo on pages 138–139.

• You could also bake this recipe in a loaf pan and make banana bread!

Everyday Egg Bolos

It's because of the people in your life, who encourage you, make you laugh, and give you strength, that you're able to be at your best every day. But instead of doing something embarrassingly extravagant to show your gratitude, how about making these simple egg bolos? The soft, sweet taste that melts in your mouth makes them the perfect little gift for an ordinary day.

Egg Bolos Recipe

Ingredients

- 1 egg yolk
- ¼ cup (25 g) powdered sugar
- ⅓ cup (50 g) cornstarch
- 1 tbsp (15 ml) skim milk
- 1 tbsp (15 ml) ground black sesame seeds
- 1 tsp (5 ml) water

Directions (makes 50 pieces)

1. Preheat the oven to 325°F (170°C).
2. Whisk the egg yolk and powdered sugar together well.
3. Add the cornstarch, skim milk, sesame seeds and water to the mixture from step 2, then knead. *Note: You want the texture to be smooth and about ¼" (6 mm) thick; add/adjust the amount of cornstarch and water if necessary.*
4. Once the dough reaches the proper texture, tear pieces from it and roll them into round balls, about ½" (13 mm) in size.
5. Place on a baking sheet and bake for about 12 minutes.

Rolling the balls up one by one is time-consuming, but well worth the effort!

♟ Tasty Tips

• I added black sesame seeds to give the egg bolos a slightly more mature flavor. You could also use white sesame seeds or leave them plain.

• Since these cookies easily dissolve in one's mouth, even small children and babies can enjoy them.

You could also knead the dough into a ½"-diameter (13 mm) stick, then cut into ½"-wide (13 mm) pieces..

These are cute too!

🎁 When Giving as a Gift

• Arrange the egg bolos in a lunch box, along with a pack of herbal tea. If you put the time into choosing a flavor of tea based on the recipient's personality, this little gift will really express your love and gratitude.

Pick a tea flavor that reminds you of the person you're giving the gift to!

Glossary

Adzuki Beans (also known as *azuki*) are a type of red bean that is often used in Japanese sweets. Available at health food stores and Asian grocers.

Anko is a sweetened red bean paste made with Adzuki Beans (see above) that is often used in Japanese desserts. It can be found in canned form at most Japanese grocers.

Awase-zu (or seasoned rice vinegar) is a mix of plain rice vinegar, sugar and salt, used to create sushi rice. It can be easily made at home, but can also just be purchased if you prefer. Found at most Asian grocers and higher-end markets.

Bamboo Shoots (*takenoko*) can be found year-round but are freshest in the spring. Available at most Asian groceries or supermarkets with an Asian-food section, and are also sold vacuum-packed and canned.

Daikon Radish is a large white radish used in lots of Asian cuisines. It's most often simmered, pickled, or added to soups. Available at Asian grocers, health food stores, and higher-end markets.

Dashi Broth is the quintessential Japanese soup stock and the base for miso soup. It is most traditionally made by soaking Kombu (see opposite) in water before simmering with bonito fish flakes. It can also be bought in granulated form, but be warned: this instant format often contains MSG. Available at Japanese and general Asian grocers.

Edamame are immature soybeans, commonly served as a finger food when boiled in their pods and sprinkled with salt. Available at most supermarkets, especially in their frozen form.

Fried Tofu Pouches (*abura age*) are made by frying thin strips of tofu; this process creates a "pocket" in the center. Commonly found in the tofu aisle of Japanese grocers, they usually come five to six sheets a pack and freeze easily (for later use).

Gobo (also known as burdock root) is a nutritious, earthy-tasting root vegetable. Its skin requires a thorough cleaning before eating, but it is recommended to eat with the peel on for its health benefits. Available at Japanese-specific grocery stores.

Japanese Mushrooms Four kinds of Japanese mushrooms are used in the recipes in this book: enoki, eringi, shiitake, and shimeji. Shiitake, being by far the most common, can be found in both fresh and dried forms at most supermarkets. All are available at Asian grocers and higher-end markets.

Japanese Rice (also called japonica or sushi rice) is a short-grain variety of white rice with a unique sticky texture. It is an integral part of Japanese cuisine. Available at most supermarkets.

Kabocha Squash is an Asian variety of winter squash. It's very sweet with bright orange flesh and a dark green skin, which is edible when cooked. Acorn and butternut squashes make for decent substitutes. Available at Asian grocers, health food stores, and higher-end markets.

Kombu is dried kelp. It's nutritious and chock-full of savory umami, and is integral in creating Japanese soup stock (see also Dashi Broth, opposite). Kombu from Hokkaido is considered the best quality. Look for white bits on the kombu itself; the more there are, the better the flavor. Available at Asian grocers, health food stores, and higher-end markets.

Lotus Root (*renkon*) is the rhizome of the lotus plant. Its crunchy texture, unique visual appeal, and health benefits make it a popular addition to stir-fries and salads. It's sold whole either with its skin or peeled (sometimes even pre-cut!), and vacuum-packed. Available at most Asian grocers.

Mirin is a common Japanese condiment. It's a sweet rice wine (albeit with negligible alcohol content) used either as a sweetener or to give a subtle sheen to fish and meat dishes. Available at most Asian grocers and supermarkets with Asian-food sections.

Mochi Rice (also known as sweet or sticky rice) is often used to create desserts, such as the chewy mochi rice cake. Available at most Asian grocers.

Myoga is a Japanese garnish that is eaten sliced thinly. Its ginger-like taste adds a refreshing quality to many dishes. Available at Japanese grocers, depending on the season.

Nori is a dried sheet of seaweed, most often used to make sushi rolls. Available at most Asian grocers, health food stores, and higher-end markets.

Panko are a type of Japanese bread crumbs. They are flaky rather than fine, resulting in an especially crunchy texture once fried. Available at most supermarkets.

Ponzu Sauce is a citrus-based dipping sauce that is often used in Japanese cooking. Available at most Asian grocers.

Rice Vinegar is a mild vinegar, ranging in color from clear to a pale yellow. It is often used for marinades and pickling, and is the base for seasoned rice vinegar, which is used to create sushi rice. Available at most supermarkets.

Sake is a Japanese rice wine. Like with sherry, a good quality, drinkable sake is recommended for cooking. Available at most liquor stores.

Satsumaimo (also called Japanese sweet potato) is identified by its reddish-purple skin and pale yellow flesh. It's sweeter and starchier than its Western counterpart. Available at Asian grocers and higher-end markets.

Sea Bream is a variety of fish known for its delicious and mild white meat. Available at your local fish monger, higher-end markets, and Japanese grocers with a seafood section.

Shichimi translates to "seven flavor chili pepper" and is a popular Japanese seasoning that can be found at most Asian grocers.

Shiso Leaf is a common Japanese garnish that comes in green and red varieties. It can be found fresh at Japanese grocers.

Soy Sauce (*shoyu*) is a popular soy-based flavoring, ubiquitous in much of Asian cuisine. Because it is such an important cooking component, it is recommended to invest in a higher-quality version. Available at most supermarkets.

Tofu is soybean curd. It's very healthy due to being low in calories and protein rich. It comes in different varieties, most commonly firm and silken. Available at most supermarkets.

Tonkatsu Sauce is often described as a Japanese Worcestershire sauce (which can be used as a substitute, though it does vary a little in taste and consistency). It is most often poured over or used as a dip for fried food. Available at most Asian grocers.

Ume Plums are most often used to make either plum wine (*umeshu*) or pickled plums (*umeboshi*). Fresh ume plums are only available for a short window of time (usually from May to June), even in Japan, and getting ahold of them outside of Japan proves to be a bigger challenge. Available in-store and by mail order at Mitsuwa, the Japanese-grocery chain (see Resources, pages 149–150).

Wasabi (also known as Japanese horseradish) is a very spicy accompaniment to many Japanese dishes, most notably sushi. It's most commonly found in paste and powder forms, though it can be bought fresh. Available at Japanese grocers and supermarkets with an Asian section.

Yamaimo (also known as *nagaimo* or Chinese mountain yam) is an extremely healthy yam with a distinct sticky texture when peeled. Its flesh has been known to cause itchy skin for some people, so be careful when handling it with your bare hands. Available at most Asian grocers.

Yuzu is a Japanese citrus lemon with an aromatic peel and juice that can be described as tasting somewhere between a grapefruit and a lime. It is in-season throughout the winter. Available at most Asian grocers, which also sell bottled yuzu juice.

Resources

Japanese Cooking Websites

Japanese Cooking 101
(japanesecooking101.com)

Just Hungry
(justhungry.com)

Savory Japan
(savoryjapan.com)

Japanese Grocers: Online

Asian Food Grocer
(asianfoodgrocer.com)

Japan Super
(japansuper.com)

Marukai e-store
(marukaiestore.com)

Rakuten
(global.rakuten.com)

Suzuki Farm
(nihonyasai.com)

Japanese Grocers: Locations

Canada

Fujiya Japanese Foods (4 locations; fujiya.ca)
912 Clark Drive, Vancouver, BC
(604) 251-3711

#112-1050 W. Pender Street, Vancouver, BC
(604) 608-1050

#113-3086 St. Edwards Drive, Richmond, BC
(604) 270-3715

3624 Shelbourne Street, Victoria, BC
(250) 598-3711

Heiwa Oriental Market
7018 Chebucto Road, Halifax, NS
(902) 455-8383

Komatsu Japanese Market (sushikelowna.com)
140-1855 Kirschner Road, Kelowna, BC
(250) 862-9338

United States
East Coast
Dainobu (2 locations; dainobu.us)
129 E. 47th Street, New York, NY
(212) 755-7380

36 W. 56th Street, New York, NY
(212) 707-8525

Family Market
29-15 Broadway, Astoria, NY
(718) 956-7925

Fuji Mart
1212 E. Putnam Avenue, Greenwich, CT
(203) 698-2107

Katagiri (katagiri.com)
224 E. 59th Street, Suite A, New York, NY
(212) 755-3566

Midoriya
167 N. 9th Street, Brooklyn, NY
(718) 599-4690

Mitsuwa Marketplace (mitsuwa.com)
595 River Road, Edgewater, NJ
(201) 941-9113

Nijiya Market (nijiya.com)
18 North Central Avenue, Hartsdale, NY
(914) 949-2178

Nippan Daido (daidomarket.com)
522 Mamaroneck Avenue, White Plains, NY
(914) 683-6735

Sunrise Mart (3 locations)
29 Third Avenue, New York, NY
(212) 598-3040

12 E. 41st Street, New York, NY
(646) 380-9280

494 Broome Street, New York, NY
(212) 219-0033

West Coast
Ebisu Supermarket
18930 Brookhurst Street, Fountain Valley, CA
(714) 962-2072

Imahara Produce
19725 Stevens Creek Boulevard, Cupertino, CA
(408) 257-5636

Japantown Shopping Mall (sfjapantown.org)
San Francisco, CA

Marukai Market (marukai.com)
8 locations in Southern California

Mitsuwa Marketplace (mitsuwa.com)
7 locations in California

Nijiya Market (nijiya.com)
10 locations in California

Takahashi Market (takahashimarket.com)
221 S. Claremont Street, San Mateo, CA
(650) 343-0394

Uwajimaya (uwajimaya.com)
4 locations in Oregon and Washington

Midwest
Koyama Shoten (koyama-shoten.com)
37176 6 Mile Road, Livonia, MI
(734) 464-1480

Mitsuwa Marketplace (mitsuwa.com)
100 E. Algonquin Road, Arlington Heights, IL
(847) 956-6699

Sakura Mart (sakuramart.com)
8640 Haines Drive, Suite C, Florence, KY
(859) 918-5026

Tensuke Market (tensukemarket.com)
1167 Old Henderson Road, Columbus, OH
(614) 451-6002

Tensuke Market-Chicago (tensuke-chicago.com)
3 S. Arlington Heights Road, Elk Grove Village, IL
(847) 806-1200

South
Asahi Imports (asahi-imports.com)
6105 Burnet Road, Austin, TX
(512) 453-1850

Nippan Daido (daidomarket.com)
11146 Westheimer Road, Houston, TX
(713) 785-0815

Shop Minoya
3115 W. Parker Road, Plano, TX
(972) 769-8346

What Is Furoshiki?

A furoshiki is a a traditional Japanese wrapping cloth that has been used for hundreds of years—since the Muromachi Period (1392–1573). You can think of it as being the original tote bag!

Furoshiki can be used to tie up and carry any number of items, including boxes, gifts, and bottles. They are convenient and eco-friendly, and are now available in both traditional and modern styles. They are also the perfect way to transport your little gifts, as the furoshiki can be presented as part of the gift you are giving. Here are some websites to help you learn more about furoshiki:

Furochic (furochic.com)

Furoshiki (furoshiki.com)

Furoshiki Kyoto (shop.furoshiki.co.jp)

LuLu Wraps (luluwraps.com)

Myfuroshiki (myfuroshiki.blogspot.com)

Uguisu (uguisu.ocnk.net)

About the Author

wato was born in Iwate, Japan, and is a nutritionist, food stylist and illustrator. She is active in a wide variety of media, including the popular Japanese magazines *Anana* and J-Wave's *Kiss And Hug*. She also owns her own event catering business under the name wato kitchen. wato loves to cook in her free time, too! You can visit her website at blog.watokitchen.com.